Gavin Presman started his wor
brands such as Canon, Capital Radio
international trainer, speaker and insight coach. His company,
Inspire, is committed to helping businesses get more from
their people, while supporting individuals to get more from
their working lives. Clients now include many of the world's
leading media and technology businesses including Microsoft,
JCDecaux, Guardian Media Group, and Twitter.

He is a Master Practitioner of NLP, a Master Trainer and
EMEA Partner for Lumina Learning, a graduate and former
coach on Landmark Education's Curriculum for Living, and
a graduate of both the One Thought and Insight Principle's
Professional Institutes.

As an Associate of the Innate Health Centre (IHC) he is
committed to bringing a greater understanding of the human
operating system into schools. He is also committed to his
role as a mentor at The House of St Barnabas, an innovative
charity and members club in London that support those impacted by homelessness back into work. Gavin also speaks at
music festivals to families about how to experience more love
through an understanding of our 'Human Operating System'.
He is also Chair of Governors at Eden Primary, a free school he
helped to found.

He lives in London with his wife, Jools, and his three children. You can get in touch with him on @gavinpresman or
gavin@inspire-ing.co.uk.

how to: ACADEMY launched in September 2013. Since then it
has organized over 400 talks and seminars on Business, Lifestyle, and Science & Technology, which have been attended by
40,000 people. The aim of the series is to anticipate the needs
of the reader by providing clarity, precision and know-how in
an increasingly complex world.

GAVIN PRESMAN

HOW TO: SELL WITH COMPLETE CONFIDENCE

bluebird
books for life

First published 2017 by Bluebird
an imprint of Pan Macmillan
20 New Wharf Road, London N1 9RR
Associated companies throughout the world
www.panmacmillan.com

ISBN 978-1-5098-1443-5

Copyright © How To Academy Limited 2017

The right of Gavin Presman to be identified as the
author of this work has been asserted by him in accordance
with the Copyright, Designs and Patents Act 1988.

All rights reserved. No part of this publication may be reproduced,
stored in a retrieval system, or transmitted, in any form, or by any means
(electronic, mechanical, photocopying, recording or otherwise)
without the prior written permission of the publisher.

Pan Macmillan does not have any control over, or any responsibility for,
any author or third-party websites referred to in or on this book.

9 8 7 6 5 4 3 2 1

A CIP catalogue record for this book is available from the British Library.

Printed and bound by CPI Group (UK) Ltd, Croydon, CR0 4YY

This book is sold subject to the condition that it shall not, by way of
trade or otherwise, be lent, hired out, or otherwise circulated without
the publisher's prior consent in any form of binding or cover other than
that in which it is published and without a similar condition including
this condition being imposed on the subsequent purchaser.

Visit **www.panmacmillan.com** to read more about all our books
and to buy them. You will also find features, author interviews and
news of any author events, and you can sign up for e-newsletters
so that you're always first to hear about our new releases.

*This book is dedicated to the
most persuasive gang I know,
my gorgeous children
Yasmin, Ziggy and Saffron.
I really hope you don't read it,
because you know too much
about influence already.
I love you beyond what
my mind can understand,
and will forever.*

Contents

INTRODUCTION – WHY WE NEED A NEW WAY OF LOOKING AT AN OLD ART

Many years ago, working as a sales manager for a radio station in central London, I got my assistant, Ellie, into serious trouble with her mother when I let slip that she was working in my team. She was convinced that her daughter's job was passing records to the DJ rather than helping to pay his wages. While this may seem trivial, it uncovers an attitude to sales that permeates much of society today, and one that this book aims to transform. Ellie wanted to avoid being associated with the sales profession for the same reason as many other people: she felt uncomfortable with the idea of selling. But selling is a fundamental and critical part of any business, and the skills and processes involved are useful for everyone who wants to make a difference in his or her world.

How to: sell with complete confidence will show how selling is not only a critical part of every business, but a critical part of every society. We need to trade products, services and ideas in order to create the world we want, and we need the skills to be able to do that effectively and ethically. Having spent the last twenty-five years of my life training salespeople, it is clear to me that one of the most critical barriers to selling is the attitude that it is somehow distasteful or dishonest. In order to learn the skills necessary to convince anyone to buy anything, we first need to adopt a new attitude towards selling, one that is positive and practical, and sees selling as what it is: an opportunity to help another human being make a decision about a product, service or idea in a way that serves them best.

Everybody is a salesperson

Whatever you do in life, the ability to sell is a useful skill to have. Understanding what it takes to change another person's mind is a prerequisite for getting things done – and everyone in business needs to get things done. Being able to get someone to say 'yes' or 'no' to an idea, an activity, or a purchase is critical. And, of course, outside of business it is equally important to be able to use your skills of persuasion. Whether it is getting your children to eat spinach or your grandmother to come snowboarding, the ability to get a 'yes' is an art that helps us in every area of our lives.

In a book that has highlighted a new approach to selling, *To Sell Is Human*,[1] Daniel Pink argues that whatever our profession, in order to get results we need sales skills. For example, when I go and see my osteopath, there are two things that will produce results for me. Firstly, her understanding of my physical condition and ability to adjust my spine accordingly. Secondly, her sales skills. If she is able to sell me the idea of further treatment together with the exercises and lifestyle changes that will create lasting change, then we are both winners. If she fails to convince me of the need for follow-up sessions and real action outside the treatment room, then the visit is unlikely to have much value for me, or for her business.

And it is not only those running traditional businesses who need these skills of persuasion. In our 'How to Sell

Anything' sessions at the How to: Academy in London I never cease to be amazed by the variety of people who are able to benefit from fine-tuning their commercial skills: artists, sculptors, bankers, interior designers, writers, consultants, teachers, agents and actors have all seen that developing 'sales skills' produces results in their professional and personal lives. And because selling depends on natural human communication skills, by honing these we enhance our ability to produce results in all areas of our lives.

You don't need to be scared of selling

Our fear of selling comes from a mistrust of certain salespeople. In the UK it is often estate agents or car insurance and double-glazing salespeople who are viewed as dishonest and devious. We therefore see the activity of selling as somehow dirty, and some of us are even convinced that the ability to deceive is a core skill for a salesperson.

This could not be further from the truth. Few of the businesses I work with today could survive if they weren't able to have long-term relationships with their customers. Whether you are selling art or ideas, if you don't sell the right thing to the right person, you are unlikely to build a relationship or create the long-term sales pipeline that will make your business a success. It is interesting to note that 'cut-throat selling' is no longer seen as appropriate.

The reality is that you can't force people to change their beliefs. You may be able to bully someone into making a quick decision in the moment, but human beings are complex creatures. When we have been coerced we quickly experience 'buyer's remorse' – the feeling that someone has taken advantage of us and pushed us into buying something we don't need or want – which often leads to a desire to reverse our decision. You have probably experienced buyer's remorse at some point, and this will contribute to your fear of the sales process. The feeling is so common that when we make certain contracts, consumer legislation allows us a period of time to change our minds. However, more common than buyer's remorse is what I call 'seller's remorse', which is an understanding by the salesperson that they have done something to put the buyer off, by interrupting his or her decision-making process.

THINK ABOUT THIS: Have you ever been part way through a buying process when your intuition has told you that the salesperson doesn't really have your interests at heart? It may be as simple as walking into a shop and getting a 'bad vibe' from the sales operation, or you may be in a one-to-one conversation when you decide to walk. What did you do? Chances are that, like thousands of people I've polled, you have walked away from buying a product you wanted because you felt uncomfortable about the person selling it.

Believe in what you are selling

There is a simple truth about selling. If you fail to have the other party's interest at heart, you risk short-term, and long-term, failure. If you are looking to sell products you don't believe in, or a service that has no value, then I'm afraid this book isn't going to help you. You can't really, without deceiving the customer, sell stuff that's of little or no value. The good news is that most of us don't need to do that, and because we live in such a global economy, it is easy for us to find the people who do have a genuine need for the products or services that we offer.

This point is important so, if you don't mind, I'm going to labour it. You can't use the following tools and techniques unless you believe that what you are selling has real value. And that in itself is quite liberating. You can't really influence a sale unless you are doing so with a positive intent. At least that's how I, and thousands of people I have met and trained, see it. Selling is no more than the process of finding out if the person with whom you are interacting really needs your product or service – and then helping them to see that for themselves.

This positive mindset is critical to your success. You need to both believe in your product or service, and communicate that belief. When we understand that selling, done correctly, is both a natural and satisfying activity, we realize that there are so many other areas in which we can produce better results by using our powers of persuasion.

TRY THIS NOW: The fact is that sometimes this positive mindset gets lost beneath the pressure of trying to produce results. Put yourself in your customer's shoes and consider how it will benefit them to do business with you. When I encounter a salesperson who is struggling to produce results, I often ask them to connect with existing customers and ask them to explain how they use the product (or service) and what benefits they experience. If you stop now and do this, you will see the situation in new ways. Pick up the phone and call someone who uses your service. It may be someone who hasn't bought the product from you. It maybe a customer of your competitor – it doesn't matter. Until you are deeply connected with the value you are offering, you will struggle to articulate the benefits to potential customers.

Beyond 'Always Be Closing'

My early sales career was in the market trade, and I was privileged in my teens to work alongside some of the most creative and effective salespeople in the world, including a lovely couple, Dave and Hazel, who sold kitchen slicers and car polish to 'punters' at Wembley Market, in the shadow of the now fallen Wembley Towers. I watched in awe as their carefully crafted pitches mesmerized crowds. They wove stories into their sales 'spiels' that spoke to the customers' unfulfilled needs, and uncovered desires they never knew they had. Years of working with Dave and Hazel served as a valuable apprenticeship for me in the world of selling, and I learnt not only the art of resilience, but also the importance of real human connection, and positive intent in the sales process.

Years later, having left school with only a few O levels, I longed for a more 'professional' sales career so I donned a suit and set about selling photocopiers and fax machines.

Little did I realize that at the time, the late 1980s, most photocopier salespeople didn't share the beliefs about selling that I now hold. My mentors were better versed in the 'old-school' tools of persuasion. Gripped by the greed that drove Thatcher's Britain, they taught me some cruel and unsavoury lessons. They believed that people needed to be 'pushed', and the motto ABC (Always Be Closing) was the call of the day. Pushing people did involve an element of understanding customers' needs, but ultimately the focus was always on 'closing', and closing at any cost. There are still pockets of these kinds of salespeople around, and they give the business a bad name, contributing to the discomfort many of us experience when things are being sold to us. Fortunately, they are in the minority and there is now a more effective, and enjoyable, sales methodology.

The new ABC: Attunement, Buoyancy and Clarity

Daniel Pink introduced me to a new ABC for selling: Attunement, Buoyancy and Clarity.

In *To Sell Is Human* he demonstrates what Dave and Hazel always knew, that tuning in with the customer, staying positive and being clear are far more useful tools. This is because the world has changed. People are no longer reliant on you, as a salesperson, to get information about your product or service. The Internet means that consumers can easily obtain information on our products and services from the web, and find our competitors there as well. It is necessary for us to take a different approach, now that the customer is in control of the information flow.

Attunement – We have to deeply understand the motivations, wants and needs of our customers, and we must tune into those needs in order to take a positive role in influencing their buying decisions.

Buoyancy – We need to ensure we stay buoyant and positive about our role in the process.

Clarity – Finally, consumers need us to be clear. It is important for us to know how to articulate our message in a simple and effective way if we are to be heard above all the other noise.

Many of the tools and techniques I will introduce to you have been proven over hundreds of years, but the positive mindset of the professional salesperson defines our age. The shift from Always Be Closing to Attunement, Buoyancy and Clarity is one that will support you in the long term.

Why are you in sales?

I ask participants on my training courses to put up their hands if they dreamed of a career in sales as a child, and I rarely get more than a smattering of hands. In fact, hands hardly ever go up. And yet many of us need to sell ideas, products or services in order to help our business to succeed. Without a positive attitude towards the sales process and an understanding of how to help someone make a buying decision, this is a hard job to do. Fortunately, both the attitude and the actions are easy to learn. In over twenty-five years as a salesman, sales manager and sales trainer I have helped thousands of people adopt the right behaviours to make the job easy, enjoyable and effective.

These behaviours don't only help buyers make decisions

with real confidence, they enable salespeople to operate with it too. I look forward to helping you do the same.

> **TRY THIS NOW:** The real value from *how to: sell with complete confidence* will come when you begin to apply the insights you have learnt. In order to make this easier, I have created some exercises to help you reflect on your success. Get yourself a notebook and keep it to hand in order to record your answers and thoughts. This notebook will become a useful reminder of what you are learning and will help you make the small behavioural changes that can produce results.

1:

THE PSYCHOLOGY OF SELLING

The first lesson for any ethical salesperson is to work out why people buy. In order to do this it's worth considering basic human psychology. Why do humans do anything? The psychologist Abraham Maslow spent a lifetime exploring this idea. He concluded that we primarily do things because we are seeking to meet unfulfilled needs, and suggested that once our more basic needs as humans are met then other 'higher level' unmet needs kick in. He proposed a hierarchy of needs in which our most basic needs sit at the bottom of the pyramid.

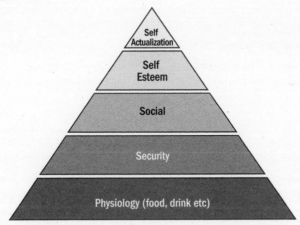

As the illustration above shows, our most basic needs are for security, social interaction, self-esteem, self-fulfilment and, finally, self-actualization. What Maslow suggested was that a human without any unfulfilled needs literally does nothing. Think about it, it will probably prove true for you.

Maslow illustrated his thesis by talking about early human groups wandering the plains looking for food. The primary needs of the tribe were for food and drink. Once they had food (let's say they killed a buffalo), the focus would move to finding water and then shelter. As soon as a shelter was found (let's say they found a cave), and a fire was built, the effort would turn to fulfilling social needs. Socializing – finding friends – would then become the priority, and then a new need would kick in: the need for self-esteem. Maslow proposed that as soon as we had found friends, our focus would turn to feeling better than the others, or at least feeling good about ourselves. Only when this is satisfied do we start looking to meet the more esoteric needs, such as to feel fulfilled, or, as Maslow put it, 'actualized'. This hierarchy of needs is simply a theory that points towards how humans are motivated to act. In a nutshell, Maslow suggested that every human action is the 'activation' of an unfulfilled need.

What does that mean for us as salespeople? Well, it's simple. An active part of the sales process is to help the buyer to appreciate, and then realize, their unfulfilled needs. A sales process is unsuccessful when the buyer or the salesperson is not connected to a real, unfulfilled need.

Coca-Cola demonstrate this in advertising. What unfulfilled needs could be met by their products? You would think the need Coca-Cola meets would be at the bottom of the pyramid: the need for a drink. Have you ever seen an ad that reads, *Drink Coke – it will stop you being thirsty*? No. Coca-Cola appreciate that if we are in need of a drink, this could be met by any of their competitors or simply by a glass of water. So they point you, through their advertising, towards the fulfilment of more sophisticated needs. Coca-Cola imply that their product will help consumers meet social needs, or even the need for self-esteem. The message in Coke adverts is: *Drink Coke and you'll be part of the Coke community. Therefore you will have more friends.*

So why is this important for us to understand? Well, sales is the process of fulfilling unmet human needs. Therefore a salesperson's job is not simply to present the features and benefits of a product. It is to help the customer appreciate and explore their unmet needs, and then to show the customer how the product or service can help them to meet those needs. Salespeople who understand this distinction spend much of their energy uncovering customers' needs, rather than talking about their product. Until a customer really appreciates what needs they are seeking to fulfil, they are rarely in a place to make a decision.

This understanding unites all kinds of selling. On a practical level, there are a host of differences between selling products, services and consultancies. First and foremost, with products you have something physical to show the customer, and with services and consultancies you are often only able to show the result of what someone else bought. However, fundamentally the process is the same. A human being is faced with a set of unmet needs; they must decide on how to meet those needs, and they will buy based on whether they believe that their needs are important enough to justify the expenditure and that your product or service will meet those needs.

With this understanding we come to a definition of selling:

Selling is a two-way conversation, aimed at discovering the customer's unmet needs and showing how your product or service can meet these needs by creating a desire to buy.

With this definition in mind, 'closing' becomes a natural part of the process rather than the primary goal. People who understand that you can fulfil their needs do not need to be 'closed', although, as we will see later on, there are things that you can do to help them recognize what their needs might be.

Understanding the buyer's state of mind

Do you ever wonder why it is that on some days when you go out shopping, regardless of your intention, you buy more things than other days? Why do you sometimes feel in more of a 'buying mood'? As a salesperson, understanding this is important because it gets results. Interestingly, in street markets it is understood that on windy days we are less likely to buy. It's simply because we don't like being 'pushed around', and often that's exactly what the wind does. If you are trying to get people to stand still for ten minutes to watch a demonstration of a product, the feeling of being manipulated by the wind is distracting. It makes you feel uncomfortable, and feeling uncomfortable is an inbuilt sign that you shouldn't make decisions.

This sensation isn't much different from feeling pushed around mentally. Human beings value independent thought, and so the moment we sense we are being bullied, our defences go up and we stop feeling comfortable. Ultimately we want people to make their buying decisions in a space where they are feeling comfortable, and so it's worth understanding how people's moods work, and what can influence these moods.

The first thing to say here is that we often misunderstand where our feelings come from. Most people believe that their feelings are a reflection of circumstances and that other people and situations cause feelings and are therefore responsible for their state of mind. This is not true. Our feelings are not our circumstances but the result of our thinking. We create feelings from the inside, through the power of thought.

Therefore, it's important to pay attention to the buyer's state of mind. Anyone in a low mood is unlikely to be able to think clearly and make the right decision. Remember that moods change constantly, so paying attention to the client's feelings and thinking is as important as paying attention to what they are actually saying.

Great salespeople are not only alert to their customers' state of mind. They also create an environment where the customer is able to make a clear and confident decision.

This is where my philosophy differs from many of the 'sales systems' that are being peddled on the market today. While I am sure that people do need to connect with unmet needs, I am not convinced that it is your job to exaggerate or stress the bad feelings that can occur when we think about unmet needs. In a system called SPIN Selling, we are encouraged to not only explore the Situation and the Problem the customer faces, but to dig deep into the Implications and paint a picture of what will happen if the Need remains unfulfilled.[2] We then show how we can meet that Need. Such systems may be extremely popular in business, but my issue with them is that they focus too much on the negative side of unmet needs. I'm not saying that SPIN selling doesn't work, but it doesn't need to be that complex, and it's not necessary to generate negative states in our customers in order to get results. I'm suggesting the opposite: that we should focus on creating positive states. Once the bruise is pressed, I believe you can easily paint a positive picture of the benefit for the customer.

Managing your own state of mind

It is clear to anyone who has tried selling anything for a period of time that one of the biggest factors in success is your own state of mind. In my early days as a sales trainer in the local newspaper business, I perfected the art of predicting a team member's sales results by spending less than three minutes simply watching him or her working. I was able to determine whether a person was having a 'good selling day' (in this case in a telesales environment) by simply observing body language and looking for clues to his or her personal state of mind. One reason that our training at Inspire often produces extraordinary results for salespeople who have previously experienced a 'sales slump' is that we focus first on getting our participants into the right state of mind.

How can we do this? When we understand that a bad mood means that we are caught in a downward spiral by our own thinking, it is easy to get back to a positive and balanced state of mind. We will talk more about how to do this in the following chapters, but for now it's useful to see the effect that our thinking can have on results.

The trick to managing your own state of mind is not to learn a number of positive affirmations, or to create a routine of diet or exercise. Clearly diet and exercise are helpful elements for a healthy lifestyle, and for some people positive affirmations can create temporary mood changes. However, the most effective lesson for me was to simply learn how my mental system really worked. Once you have a genuine understanding of the below two principles, you have an instant reset button that works without having to press anything.

1. Our reality is dependent on our thought processes.

2. We experience thought through our consciousness, and at any given time we will have a different experience of our thought, depending on our current level of consciousness.

While our moods will always fluctuate, what is guaranteed is that beyond our conscious thought lie powers of creativity and innovation. These unconscious powers I'll call Mind, but over the years there have been plenty of ways to try and describe them. Recently I experienced a live demonstration of Mind. At the Edinburgh Festival I enjoyed a performance of a comedy format called 'Hyprov', where members of the audience are hypnotized and then take part in a live improvised show. It was incredible to see the wit, skill and acting abilities demonstrated by the participants when they allowed the unconscious mind to take over. Having studied and taught improvisation skills, I can understand how this works – our best ideas and innovations often come when we are allowing our unconscious mind to work, rather than relying on the limit of our personal thinking and what we already know.

Why is this useful for sales skills? Because in order to master personal Buoyancy (see Introduction, page 8), you will need to recognize that you are creating your feelings through thought, which is not an objective representation of your circumstances. Knowing this enables you to quickly reset your mood as soon as your emotional barometer tells you that you are making up some kind of unhelpful calamity. I first experienced this understanding some years ago when my father was going through a time of particularly carefree living. He told me he had been reading a book by Richard Carlson and realized that it wasn't worth 'sweating the small stuff'.[3] More importantly, he said he was seeing that it was 'all small stuff'. I discovered that Richard Carlson had been taught these useful principles by Sydney Banks, for whom 'We are only ever one thought away from a new reality'.[4]

I have found this understanding hugely helpful. When we realize the power of thought and consciousness in creating our experience, we are ready to allow our ever-powerful Mind to take over and provide us with fresh thinking, productive insights and new perspectives. I have never found much value from sweating the thoughts that permeate my everyday experience. Understanding how they work has enabled me to be far more productive and effective. As a salesperson, it helps me to see that everyone, our customers and ourselves, are only doing the best we can with the thinking we have at that time. Getting beyond moment-to-moment thinking doesn't require any more than an understanding that a new thought is on its way, and an appreciation that whenever we are feeling anxious we are rarely going to find that helpful ideas or actions follow.

I have seen that the primary focus as salespeople should be on connecting deeply with the person to whom we are selling, and appreciating our own, and our customer's state of mind is key to this. Until we are both settled and connected, it is unlikely that we will be able to genuinely discover their needs, or help them find the best way to use your product or service.

Exploring the buyer's decision-making process

In order to be a proactive part of a sales experience, you must understand where your customer is in his or her decision-making process, and how you can help them through that process. Since the 1960s, scholars have suggested that as consumers we go through a relatively similar process whenever we buy things, whether they are goods or services. This buying process is worth considering, as it can enable you to map behaviour in the sales cycle.

The traditional process is as follows:

1. The realization of a need
2. Searching for information and opinions
3. Evaluation of specific options against agreed criteria
4. Purchase
5. Post-sales evaluation

However, in my experience, there is another stage in the process. This is the 'taking some time to think about it' stage. Unless you are completely comfortable at each stage, consumers will want to hold off in order to evaluate their options before buying. In the end the model looks something like this:

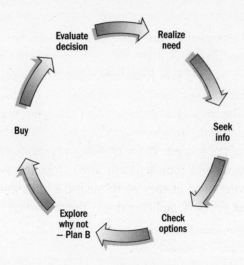

Clearly this process will work differently depending on whether you are buying an alarm clock, employing a night watch or engaging a consultant to develop a research project looking into security issues – but not incredibly differently. At some point you realize you have a need that is not being met. You are getting to work late, or losing stock overnight, or losing stock in the warehouse. You start to consider options. You ask friends, look online, look in the press and then draw up a shortlist. Once you have evaluated the options you make a decision, which will be tested depending on its seriousness. If you are buying a twenty-pound watch, I doubt you'd be doing much in the way of detailed research and feedback, but if it is a two-thousand-pound watch, you would take more information on board and seek wider opinions. There are clearly other areas to consider and opinions to canvas when employing a security firm, but the process of making the decision remains basically the same.

TRY THIS NOW: Whatever you are selling, whether it is a product, service or even an idea, use the buying process to help you understand how your customers go through their own decision-making process. Write down the six stages of the buying process in your notebook and imagine what your customer is doing at each stage of the process. You may want to break down their behaviour into four separate areas. Imagine you are observing them as they go through the buying process and ask yourself, and note down, the following:

— What are they saying at each stage? (and to whom are they saying this?)

— What are they thinking at each stage?

— What are they feeling at each stage?

— What are they actually doing at each stage?

This will give you an insight into the customer's frame of mind, their attitudes and behaviours. It will also help you suggest ways in which you may be able to support them more effectively in the process.

How does all of this help you as a salesperson? It is helpful to understand where a person is in his or her own buying process. If the buyer has already determined that he or she has a need and has therefore gathered information in preparation for making an evaluation, then you will have to accelerate your sales process to catch up. You will also have to ensure that you understand the background of your client in order to understand the criteria for making a decision.

Only then will you be able to see whether your product or service will be the right choice to meet your customer's needs.

Structuring successful sales: Prepare, Connect, Probe, Match, Agree, Close

The sales process needs to follow a similar path to the buying process. While you may be jumping in at a different stage (because there will be little preparation when you meet someone in a lift who asks you to sell them your service), it's useful to see sales as a simple process that you should be working your way through.

1. **Prepare** – Find out as much as possible about the person you are selling to and investigate what potential needs you may be able to meet. The preparation stage includes all the things you need to do to identify potential customers and discover the best way to meet and connect with them.

2. **Connect** – Introduce yourself in some way and start the process of tuning in to the potential customer as a person.

3. **Probe** – This stage is the one that is so often missed by pushy salespeople, or done in such a way that it lacks integrity or sincerity. Here we dig deep to uncover the customer's unmet needs. This is absolutely critical because a customer who doesn't recognize his or her unmet needs is unlikely to be motivated to buy. The probe does more than

discover unmet needs – it allows us to tune in to the person, generate rapport and uncover the commonality that creates unity.

4. **Match** – It is only after stages 1 to 3 that we can do what is traditionally understood as 'selling'. This stage is our opportunity to demonstrate how our product or service matches the unmet needs the customer now recognizes they have.

5. **Agree** – Once we have demonstrated the match, it's time to reach an agreement. It seems like a small thing to have its own stage in the process but this is the stage when the customer is looking for reasons not to buy. This agreement stage is critical because it enables the salesperson to help the customer work through common objections and become aligned on how the solution matches his or her requirements.

6. **Close** – The final stage is to get a 'yes', traditionally called the 'close'. As we'll see, good salespeople are getting 'yes' throughout the process, and if done right, the process naturally leads to a close. That said, many of us do operate in fiercely competitive markets and so if we don't actually secure a 'yes', and commitment to a sale, we can often leave a customer to do business with someone else. Therefore, learning how to recognize when to finally close and how to do this with comfort and conviction is a useful skill.

People that I've trained and managed seem to appreciate the idea of a sales structure because it enables them to see where they are, and to ask the right questions of themselves and their customers.

CHECKLIST

— Are you clear what previously unmet needs are being met by existing and future customers of your product or service?

— Are there more sophisticated needs that may be met in certain conditions that are not always considered in your buying or selling process?

— Are you clear about how your customers proceed through their own buying cycle and what they tend to do at each stage of the process?

— Have you asked the questions that will help you understand the customer's buying process?

— Are you clear that your feelings are not coming from your circumstances but from your thinking?

— Do you see the importance of appreciating that your thinking and not your circumstances are driving your feelings, and therefore your likelihood of being able to get the right connection to have a good conversation?

— Are you clear about how the sales structure applies to your line of work?

— Where do you usually have challenges moving through the sales structure and therefore what part of this book is likely to have most benefit for you?

2:

PREPARING FOR SUCCESS

In my early days as an office equipment salesman the trainees would be obliged to tramp the streets of central London, knocking on the doors of businesses to find out who to talk to about office needs. The process was pretty monotonous, and as we were given the target of collecting a hundred company compliment slips in a day, we would end up simply knocking on doors and asking inane questions before being fobbed off with a slip and the name of an office manager. Once we got into the business, we discovered that an early meet at Frank's Cafe would be the best way to start a 'productive day'.

First we could exchange some slips from the day before to break the back of our targets. We were then able to focus on getting more information from the places we did visit. This way, we had some good insights into the customer's business before we picked up the phone and tried to make appointments.

In my second week, however, when I was still very green, I bounded into a doctor's surgery off Harley Street completely unprepared. Far from being reluctant to engage me, the consultant's secretary looked like she had won the lottery when I told her I worked for Canon Business. Without further ado, she lunged me directly into the surgery, with a suggestion that this was perfect timing because Mr Phillips was that very morning talking about wanting to buy a photo-telex machine. Fortunately, Mr Phillips was a very kind and generous man, and he didn't throw me out when I pulled out a brochure and started trying to sell him the virtues of the new Canon Series 2 personal photocopying machine. Instead, he gently walked me by the arm into his outer office where his PA was sitting with a shiny new Canon Series 2 right beside her desk. It turned out it was a fax machine he was after. He had just returned from a trip to the States where he had seen one for the first time and he had a fantastic idea about how he could use them in the programme he was working on. Eventually I slowed right down and became engaged by Mr Phillips' story and listened to what he intended to do with these machines. He reminded me of my Uncle Joe, who also had a passion for his work and an enthusiasm for all things new.

Before I knew it, we were deeply tuned in and I really wanted to help this man demonstrate how sending X-rays via a fax machine could allow consultants to liaise with colleagues over treatment options without waiting for couriers to cross countries, or even continents. 'If I could help you prove that this would work, do you think you would buy a fax machine from me?' I asked. 'I'd buy two,' he said. That was my first commission cheque at Canon, and it all happened in just over a day. I learnt some important lessons from Mr Phillips' kindness of spirit: don't walk into a room unprepared, use every step of your way to get as much information as you can and let the customer do most of the talking, because if you can really get into their world, you are in a much better place to make things happen.

Making connections

Preparation has two key elements: find the right person, and maximize your chances of meaningful connection. The two are interrelated. In finding the right person to speak to, you have an opportunity to build your understanding of them in a way that will optimize your chances of enabling them to get what they want. This mindset – thinking how you can help them – is critical to ensuring that this stage is energizing, meaningful and productive.

Finding potential prospects in some areas isn't easy. It may seem obvious to say that your existing customers should be your first port of call. Either find new ways to help them, or get references from them for people they know that you can help. Set aside time to call your existing customer base (if you have one) to discuss what they are up to, and see if there are any extra needs, or potential references.

I was recently coaching a sales professional called Sebastian who thought his business was experiencing a slump. Falling oil prices and 'Brexit woes' had made his phone stop ringing. Also, the projects he was working on were becoming smaller, and more short-term. Adding to his woes was the recent trade fair he had attended that had produced no fresh leads, new people or projects. After a short chat and a few minutes spent playing victim, he saw that if he was going to continue to grow his business this year, he would need to take some action himself and stop blaming his circumstances for both his feelings and his business predicament. He realized that in the continuous grind to deliver projects, and with recent cutbacks in staff, he had made little contact with the people he knew in his existing customer base.

He drew up a list of twenty people to call up and connect

with, all of whom he had enjoyed speaking to in the past. He made it easy for himself by making it his goal simply to have a nice chat, ask what they were working on and share some industry information. He would also ask about the long-term impact of previous projects, and see if there were any people they might recommend him to speak to with the aim of securing future work. As Sebastian didn't want to set himself unrealistic goals, and saw himself as very busy, he only committed to calling two of these contacts per week. He therefore set off from our meeting feeling happy that he had something positive to do in order to grow his business.

Carl Jung, the father of modern psychotherapy, called positive coincidences 'synchronicity'.[5] He implied a spiritual connection between your preparation and the results that follow, but I prefer the chemist Louis Pasteur's angle that 'Chance favours a prepared mind'.[6]

Either way, one of the first people on Sebastian's list appeared on the same flight as him a few days later, so he was able to complete half of his 'homework' in the airport lounge over a gin and tonic before take-off. More excitingly, his contact not only suggested a person new to the business who was looking into some exciting new projects, but also recommended that Sebastian speak to this person's replacement in his former business. Sebastian could have finished the whole exercise then and there because those two contacts from a random conversation in Terminal 5 could have alone produced the business growth he was looking for. Fortunately, he didn't stop. Buoyed by the ease of simple conversation to generate new people to speak to and projects to work on, he ploughed through the list in just a few weeks, and was suddenly in possession of a revitalized attitude and a revitalized business.

Do you wonder how much 'luck' was really involved in Sebastian's story? Creating a list of people to call, having a clear idea of why he was calling them and a definite goal in mind enabled his conversation in the airport bar to have that much more impact. Without the list, the intention and the right mindset, the conversation would have been very different, and the outcome would have been reflective of this. It's easy to meet people you know and to talk to them, but if you have an objective and the right mindset, these conversations can be valuable for everyone.

TRY THIS NOW: Stop and think about your business and the customers who you have worked with over the past three years. If you are in a new role, think about the people you worked with in your former role, or people you have connected with in your life generally. Think of at least ten people with whom you have enjoyed conversations. People who you'd enjoy speaking to again. Write this list down. Think about what you may be able to ask them in order to connect you both with the value of the projects you worked on together. This bit is important, and it isn't only for them. It is for you. Save the list. We'll use it later. But be prepared if you meet them randomly, or are inspired to call them randomly, to have a valuable conversation – that is, a conversation that has value for both parties.

There is a useful and overly quoted truism that it takes more energy (or cash) to find a new customer than to sell to an old one. This is the case for almost every industry I work in, and for all the people I meet.

Using AIM to focus on value

A simple model I use with clients to help with preparation is called AIM, which stands for Active Information, Intention and Mindset.

Active Information

This is the critical part of AIM. Nothing makes a call or email easier to execute than the knowledge that you have something relevant and useful to talk about.

Active information is the kind that isn't obvious, or easy to discover. It is information that demonstrates that you have done some research, and have some interest in the person or the business with whom you are hoping to connect. At a simple level, if I wanted to speak to someone in the marketing team at Pret a Manger, then 'dead information' would be that they sell sandwiches, or even that they give their sandwiches away at the end of the day. This information is easy to discover and isn't anything new. However, if by visiting a store regularly I had discovered that they were experimenting with various seasonal vegetarian options, including spicy Thai summer veg rolls, then this would count as active information. While that may seem a simple example, it points to the essence of active information. It is information that you had to be active to obtain, information that demonstrates your role as someone who is actively involved in the customer's world, and information that shows that you are connected with the people, places or processes that they care about.

Active information can come from a variety of sources. These days you can programme Google Alerts to send you up-to-the-minute information on companies that you are interested in, and they will alert you whenever those companies are in the news. Information gleaned like this often feels a little two-dimensional, and so other information sources have always proved useful for me. Reading the trade press, going to exhibitions and events, and visiting the customers themselves are all good ways of gathering active information of the sort that will shift your phone conversation from a 'cold call' to something more like a 'gold call'. What turns a cold call into a gold call for me can be a simple piece of information that sparks my interest and enthusiasm, and leads me to believe that I can add value.

The act of finding out something interesting about the customer helps to create the right mindset for a constructive sales conversation.

TRY THIS NOW: Create lists of the following:

— The sources of active information that you currently use before you contact customers. (It's OK to leave this blank if it's not something you've done before.)

— Sources of active information that you may have used before, but aren't currently using.

— Sources of active information that you suspect will be useful for you.

— People who may be able to either help you find new

sources of active information, or may be sources of
active information themselves.

On the basis of the above, create a short plan to nurture
and harvest more active information for yourself.

Intention

Having discovered the people you want to connect with,
and having done your research, before making contact, you
need to be clear of your intention. It's easy to say your intention is to sell to them, but the psychology of selling suggests
that will put you both off. My suggestion is that when you
are preparing to connect with a potential customer you are
not wanting to sell. Your intention at this stage is simply to
connect and to discover whether your products or services
can meet their needs. This is important. It is now much
easier to write that letter or pick up that phone. Had Sebastian intended to sell to his existing client, he may have
clammed up when they met at the airport, and avoided the
topic altogether.

Mindset

Human beings are able to read millions of pieces of information at any given moment, but consciously process only
a fraction of this material. In *Blink*, a wonderful book on
the power of intuition, Malcolm Gladwell suggests that
we unconsciously process far more than we could ever do
consciously. He also suggests that the decisions we make
unconsciously can be statistically more robust than those we

make consciously.[7] I mention this because hiding your real mindset is something that is best left to professional poker players. When I met Mark Salem, the US forensic detective turned entertainer/mind reader, he was keen to point out that his seemingly remarkable telepathic skills were something any seven-year-old could do, 'with forty-five years of practice'. He wasn't 'reading' minds, but simply reacting to the tiny micro expressions that told him what was going on inside the brain.

> **THINK ABOUT THIS:** Have you ever had a feeling that someone is not being entirely honest with you? My kids tell me that when I am trying to wind them up, or play a joke, my expression and my tonality change ever so slightly. It is visible to them, but not noticeable to me.

Many of my clients say that they can easily tell when a sibling is lying. What is interesting is that when I ask whether anyone has ever aborted a purchase because they felt uncomfortable about the seller's integrity, while many say that they have, few can detect exactly what made them suspicious. This is because we can read non-verbal communication very well.

Take note: if you don't have the right mindset to make a sales call, then it is likely that the person on the other end of the communication will be able to tell. They may not know why, but something will be niggling them. You will be giving off clues that get in the way of making a genuine connection. If you don't want to make a sales call, then you probably shouldn't. You need to ensure that every time you pick up the phone or meet a prospective customer you are giving yourself the best chance. This means that you need to be feeling positive, confident and willing. Anything else is likely to leak through into your communication, and make it difficult to establish a real connection.

This is clearly a tall order. What if you are not well, or you have a rush of nerves as you start to hit the phone? Should you give up every time you are not feeling 100 per cent? I suspect that if everyone adopted this attitude, then very few sales calls would ever get made.

In the old days, we'd teach our participants to 'smile as you dial', and some call centres I worked with would provide mirrors for this purpose. The hypnotist Paul McKenna showed me, in an exercise I then taught for many years, how to manipulate the body's tendency to release positive endorphins when we smile and laugh. While these techniques can produce a temporary mood enhancement, once you start to see anxiety, tension and worry as the result of negative thoughts instead of feelings brought about by outside circumstances, it becomes possible to be positive at any time.

CHECKLIST

— Do you know where your future business is coming from?

— How does the prospecting pyramid work for you?

— Can you create a list of prospects?

— Can you categorize your prospects?

— Have you got a plan for how to approach your prospects?

— Are you clear about gathering active information, so that you have new and credible things to talk about with your client?

— Are you clear why you want to connect with potential contacts and does this 'intention' energize you?

— Are you clear enough now to make this call, or is your current understanding (consciousness) about how your moods work tricking you into feeling bad for some reason?

— Is there anything you can do to remind yourself of your positive intention?

— Are you genuinely curious about what your customer wants to tell you?

3:

CONNECTING

Selling requires connection, on both a physical and emotional level. The best way to really sell is to have a conversation in which you discover the customer's unmet need, and to explain how your product or service can satisfy that need.

In today's world this isn't always an easy task. Your prospective customers are often busy people and most of them, like most of you, will have a bias against speaking to salespeople. They might have a professional 'gatekeeper' such as a PA or a receptionist who helps to screen them from sales calls, or they might screen their calls themselves. In this chapter we will explore how to get through to the right person, and how to craft an introduction that will encourage your prospective customer to listen and – more importantly – to talk.

Getting past a 'gatekeeper'

There are a number of effective strategies to bypass a professional gatekeeper.

However, before we tackle these strategies, there is one thing you must bear in mind: timing. It is often easier to connect with people early and late in the day. Otherwise, over lunch, when there is often a change in staff at the switchboard, you have a better chance of being put through.

When I was doing some work for a charity's corporate fundraising team their receptionist, a wily lady with forty years' experience, gave me some useful advice. 'I can smell a salesperson,' she explained. There was no point laying on the charm; the way to prevent her interrogation was to sound so confident in your request that she wouldn't dare take the risk of not putting you through. The trick is to employ a commanding tone.

This points you towards two strategies that work in different situations. You will need to choose which one of these is best for you, and when to use it.

Strategy one: Get connected

The first strategy is to make a personal connection with the gatekeeper. This involves being honest with him or her about what you are up to, and getting them on side. Asking the gatekeeper to help schedule a conversation with the person I need to speak to has worked many times. If you are confident that you can support their business and clear about the benefit you bring, this can be the easiest approach. Simply call up and ask for their help: 'Hi, this is Gavin, calling from Inspire. I wonder if you can help me?' Then ask advice on how you might best set up a meeting or call with the right person. You will often get told to email or write in, but if you then get the gatekeeper's name, and follow up your mail a week or so later, you may find you have developed a relationship with them, and that they are able to help you to schedule the call you want.

It is worth remembering that many salespeople are not

in it for the long term, or not deeply concerned with value for their customers. Many of those calling this switchboard before or after you are in a dead-end job, pounding the phones, and will take any form of rejection as a cue to move on and redial the next prospect. If you are only calling those businesses that you are sure you can help, then it will be worth your while to follow up with an email, and to cultivate any relationship within that business that you can. Later in the process you will value the time spent doing so.

I remember one occasion when I was inspired to call a large media agency after they had won a new piece of business. Having done some business with the agency before, I had cultivated a great relationship with the receptionist and had even invited her out for drinks when I'd been entertaining. When I called up I was a little unprepared, and therefore surprised when, after briefly explaining what I wanted, she put me directly through to the CEO. While he was doubtless equally surprised to find me pitching this idea direct, he was a generous man who listened before directing me to the right account director. Having spoken to him and received his tacit approval, the subsequent meeting and proposal were far smoother for me. My point is simple. Every relationship you cultivate in a business may support you later on.

Strategy two: Act like a CEO

This second strategy is to attempt to bypass the gatekeeper by sounding so important that they feel obliged not to question you. In a large business this often works because there will be two levels of gatekeeper, a receptionist and a PA, and this will get you directly to the PA. The PA is there to support the boss, so is the best person to speak to first. Most importantly, he or she will be able to give you a number of pointers about what is going on for the manager right now, and may also be able to point you towards someone who might be better placed to speak to you. There is no golden rule here: you need to speak to as many people as possible in order to discover how best to support the organization. And remember that having the right attitude and tone will affect your likelihood of speaking to, and being heard by, the right people. Any hint of discomfort or unease with what you are doing will show in your voice, and lead to suspicion, questioning of your motives and closing down of ears, minds and telephone lines.

Subtle changes in tone will affect the way you sound and standing up when you talk impacts on both your tone and attitude. This isn't to say you need to stand up to have the right tone or attitude, but it will give your voice more resonance. This is because when you are seated your diaphragm, the muscle that pushes air into the lung and drives your speech, is restricted. Paying attention to your tone will help you sound more convincing on the phone, particularly to those who don't know you. Margaret Thatcher went through hours of vocal coaching in the 1970s in order to project sound from her diaphragm rather than her nose and mouth. This training, which singers also employ in order to deepen their tone and reduce risk of damage to the vocal cords, is a useful exercise for anyone who wants to sound more authoritative. Margaret Thatcher produced a complete turnaround in her ability to influence members of her own party by transforming how she produced her voice. I wonder whom you will be able to influence more effectively once you have a deeper, more authoritative tone?

TRY THIS NOW: See if you can notice the difference between the tones you create when you are using different parts of your body to make sound. Remember that sound is the result of the vibration of air passing through your vocal cords, but it is not only the vocal cords that create sound. The whole of your upper body is resonating when you speak, and we hear that resonance as voice. If you are largely projecting the air though your nose, mouth and throat, you will produce a very different sound than if you are using the whole of your lungs, starting at the diaphragm, to generate speech.

Try starting with a hum. See if you can hum through your nose, and then move the humming down through your mouth, your throat, your chest and even down into your belly. (If you are reading this book in a public place, you may want to wait until you get home to do this practice.) Then pay attention to the difference as you speak. Focus on moving your breath and sound to these different parts of your body. Notice how the sound generated through your nose sounds 'nasally', is thinner and a little grating. Notice how when you focus on the breath in the mouth and throat, your speech changes in quality but still lacks depth. Then notice how your tone becomes richer and deeper as you bring your attention to the chest and the diaphragm. Bringing your breath right into the depths of your lungs by using your diaphragm will produce the warmest and most attractive tone.

Avoiding 'dog words'

Under pressure or as a matter of habit, we tend to use words that follow us around and foul our speech. At Inspire we call these 'dog words'. They are words that have no meaning like 'um', 'ah', 'sort of', 'kind of', 'you know', 'obviously', 'basically' and so forth. These words can irritate potential customers; they are a sign of overthinking and can demonstrate either high levels of anxiety or low levels of confidence. Many years ago my manager would cough every time he heard me use a dog word. On the first day he did this he was coughing so much that the team thought he was sick! By drawing attention to my use of dog words, he taught me to eliminate them.

Ask for recommendations

When I sold photocopiers, I was taught a sneaky tactic that involved calling a business and asking to speak to the CEO's PA in order to get a 'recommendation'. I employed this with Alan Sugar before he was a lord (or even a sir). His PA was a little surprised that I was trying to sell photocopiers to the boss of Amstrad, but she was friendly and happy to respond when I asked whom she would 'recommend' I spoke to. When I called up that person and said I had just been talking to Alan's PA, and she 'recommended'

I speak to them, I was warmly invited in for a meeting. Interestingly, it turned out to be a waste of time because I had failed to research the fact that we were in the same business, but it taught me something useful about recommendations. They are a sure way to warm up a prospective client, and ease yourself into a position where you can have a valuable conversation.

You can employ this tactic with sincerity. Simply ask people you know, or don't know, who they would 'recommend' you speak to. When you call up that person, you will find that by simply saying 'X recommended we spoke', you start the conversation on a completely different note.

When we hear the word 'recommend' applied to someone we know and trust, we attach a great deal of weight to it. It sounds to us like the person we are speaking to has been personally recommended. If you follow up a 'recommendation' with a conversation that has genuine value, and you do this with an ethical and value-focused approach, then it will produce results for you and for others.

TRY THIS NOW: Think of three organizations you would like to sell your product to. Or if you sell to individuals, think of three people. Even if you know the main contact there, think of someone you could speak to who could offer you a 'recommendation'. You are looking for a list of people to phone in order to get recommendations of who to speak to. Try calling at least one of those people and asking for a recommendation now. Notice how easy it is. If you know no one at the organization, try calling up cold and asking at reception. Better still, use your detective skills to find the name of someone in the organization then call them up, make a human connection, and ask them who they'd recommend you speak to. Having done this exercise in hundreds of workshops, and having seen the results for myself, I'm curious about the response you get. Tweet me your responses at @gavinpresman or #howtosell. Or join the conversation in the 'how to sell with complete confidence' LinkedIn group.

Connecting virtually

Many people use their phone for looking at their social media feeds and email rather than for actually holding conversations. This is why using the telephone, particularly the landline, is more valuable now than it has ever been. When your competitors think they can conduct their business solely via email, the person who picks up the phone sometimes has the opportunity to connect with you in a deeper and more meaningful way. That said, email and social media are increasingly becoming places where people do connect, and while the intention will always be to connect in person, they are a great place to build relationships and meet new people. While there are books and courses on virtual networking, I'll share here a few ways in which people use social media to connect with prospective customers.

There is a reason why Microsoft paid $26.2 billion for LinkedIn in 2016. It provides a great way to see what people are up to, and to check them out before you connect for real. If you are in a business where many people use LinkedIn, make sure your profile is up to date and complete. Having recommendations from people who are known in your industry will help you get your strengths across, and will help those who are considering whether to connect with you. The great thing about LinkedIn is the search feature – this enables you to find out who in the company can connect you with the right person in the right place. This is primarily what I use it for. It helps me to discover who knows who, and enables me to have conversations with people who can support me. I recommend you use it in this way: not as a place to e-meet people, but as somewhere to stay connected with people you know, who can connect you to people they know.

The best way to use any social media platform is to be proactive. After you meet someone, connect with them quickly on LinkedIn. Do this personally with a message, and send a follow-up once they accept your invitation to connect. Write recommendations for others. Endorse their skills. You will soon find that they want to reciprocate. That said, if you are targeting a particular sector or business and you have someone in your network who you know is respected in that area, ask them specifically for a recommendation. You may even want to help them by drafting it yourself. Then ensure that this recommendation is visible in your profile before you try making connections in that industry or organization. It will help the person you are connecting with to trust you, if you are being recommended by someone they trust already.

TRY THIS NOW: Look at a few LinkedIn profiles of people in organizations or sectors that you target. Look at what feels trustworthy to you. What works and doesn't work? Now look at your own profile. Make a list of five things you could add to or take away from your profile to make it easier for people to want to connect with you. Make a plan to put these ideas into action.

LinkedIn isn't the only social network that can help you connect with prospective clients – it's just the one I am most familiar with for that purpose. I tend to use Facebook for family and friends, but the capacity to connect and build relationships on Facebook is clearly evident. More recently I've allowed a few select clients and contacts into my Facebook world and it is interesting to see how this adds depth to our connection. Twitter can also support you, as long as it's only a small part of your effort. Meeting people for real will always provide the most direct opportunity to connect.

Networking face to face

Most industries provide many opportunities in which to network and meet new people. If you tell yourself that you are simply planning to meet people who can help you to help others, then you will have a better time and see better results. You don't want to find yourself selling at parties or industry events, when you could be getting to know people instead. If the conversation does turn to your product or service, my advice is to steer them towards a separate meeting, or arrange a phone conversation to follow up. That is not a blanket ban on selling over a drink, but a suggestion that selling, and connecting, is easier once you know the person. If you spend your social life being sociable, then you can spend your professional life reconnecting with people you met when you were out and about.

Handing out business cards is useful, but my suggestion is that in order to create better connections, when you have met someone you would like to meet again you should find a reason to follow up. It may be to send them something, or to introduce them to someone you know. As long as you do it with a good heart, and without expecting immediate return, you'll build a network of people to call on when you need an introduction, or some help.

A friend called Tom recently told me a wonderful story about Bill Clinton. During his presidency Tom was introduced to Clinton at a small reception and they had a brief chat. An A-list Hollywood film star then joined them and when Clinton introduced Tom to the film star, he said, 'I really want you to meet Tom, he runs a business that does x, y, z . . .'

It not only shocked Tom that Bill Clinton had remembered his name, but by introducing him in this way he felt special, and included. If you can do this when you are out at events – introduce people to other people – you will find you become better connected yourself.

Connect with the 'three Cs': credentials, credibility, curiosity

When you speak with someone you don't know, you have very little time to establish a connection. This is even more the case over the phone. You need to ensure that anything you say in the first few seconds is primarily focused on building trust and curiosity. While much of this will be done through your tone and attitude, your words also really count. You alone will know what is the right thing to say, that any script sounds worn the second time you say it, but there is a tried and tested formula to prepare yourself. Knowing that you have to establish credentials, credibility and curiosity in only twenty to thirty seconds can help you craft something that is just right.

You need to ensure you don't rush, or say anything that implies you don't value your own time. This is an easy mistake to make. Apologizing, or mentioning that you don't want to waste their time, can do this. Be clear, be calm, and be committed.

Personally, I always want to ensure that it is a good time to talk before I say much more than hello. I do that by asking. And I use the same phrase now that I've used for years, because it really works. 'Is now a good time to talk?' It works because while it allows the other party the chance to say no, it implies that there will be a good time to talk, and demonstrates your respect. You may find yourself put off on numerous occasions with a 'no', but if you ask when there might be a better time, and then follow this up, your conversation will have started off on the right foot.

Credentials – Establishing your credentials is easy. Tell them who you are, and the company you are calling from.

Credibility – You need to reflect on the purpose of your call, using the AIM principles from Chapter 2 (see page 30). Establish your intention and the active information you have about the person or organization. Your intention is to have a conversation of value, so remember that you have something of value to offer. Do not focus too much on your proposition in your opening words. Having a clear mindset is also useful, but most importantly, show you have done your homework. Using your active information wisely at this point will increase your credibility.

The easiest way to establish credibility is through a recommendation. Another way is to mention projects that you are working on, or have worked on. That said, it is important never at this point to say anything that breaks the confidentiality of existing client relationships. Focusing on the big picture, with your eye on the results, is far safer than trying to talk about what you are doing in what could be a competitive marketplace.

Curiosity – However, it is key for your introduction to generate curiosity. This means encouraging the other person to want to hear more. If you say too much, or talk too much about what you are doing, you are unlikely to produce this effect. By contrast, if you talk about the benefits you are creating, the person may become curious. This balance of inspiring curiosity without saying too much is key. You only have a few seconds to inspire the person to want to engage in a conversation. Choosing your words carefully, and not saying too much, is the best way to do this.

The challenge with writing scripts for a sales call is that as soon as they are written they become stale, and anything read aloud sounds wooden. That's why I recommend that you write out roughly what you'd like to say when you are making a first call, but that you never use it as a script. Throw it away, pick up the phone and talk for real. It is enough to use this formula to determine what you'd like to get across. With the right intention and the right mindset, you will easily connect with prospective customers, and begin conversations of value.

TRY THIS NOW: If you are planning to call people you don't know in order to start a valuable conversation, then this will be a useful exercise for you. If you don't intend to speak to perfect strangers, you may not find it so useful.

Write a script (that you will throw away) to cover the first twenty seconds of a call with a prospective customer. Try to craft it so that you get across who you are (credentials). Try to generate credibility and curiosity. Get out your smartphone and speak it into a recording app. Play it back to yourself. Give yourself some feedback. Do you really sound credible? Would you be curious if you were on the other end of the phone? What could you improve about the delivery to demonstrate your value and confidence? What clearly worked for you that you would want to repeat in a real call? Do it once more, this time without looking at your script. Now play it back and give yourself feedback again using the questions above.

Try this for a different customer. See if you can change the approach and find different ways to establish credibility and curiosity. The more you do this, the easier it will be for you to approach new customers on the phone and create genuine connections that lead to sales.

CHECKLIST

— Are you clear about your preparation, and are you feeling confident?

— Do you have active information, and the right intention and mindset?

— Have you used your network to find a person you can genuinely say has recommended you?

— Are you relaxed and feeling clear about the value you can bring to others?

— Are you speaking clearly and with control, using an authoritative tone?

— Are you speaking without apology, or 'dog words'?

— Have you thought through how you will establish credibility, by using examples or recommendation?

— How will you use the active information you learnt in your preparation to build credibility?

— Have you decided how you will create curiosity without saying too much about your product or service?

4:

DISCOVERING NEEDS

Aged thirteen, I entered the world of sales in Wembley Market because I had been told I had the 'gift of the gab'. I was arrogant and articulate, and those seemed to be the ideal ingredients for a sales career. It took me a long time to realize that these qualities are often more of a barrier to selling than an aid. I will show you in this chapter how the most important tools in the art of selling are questioning combined with skilled listening.

Recently I was disturbed during some gardening by a salesperson from my TV and telephone provider. She was hyped up and keen to sell me an enhanced TV package. She wasn't interested in me at all, but her script called for her to ask some questions about my TV consumption in order to 'discover' my need for more TV. While I was clearly busy, and told her as much, it was amusing for me to let her continue, as I suspected she might be able to provide some material for the participants of my courses or readers of my books. Having told her that I only watch documentaries, cooking programmes and catch-up of football highlights, she launched into her pitch. Ignoring the fact that I had told her that I don't watch films at home, she was keen to push the extra film packages and sports channels in the 'Premium' selection. She told me I would be rewarded for my 'loyalty' in buying all this extra stuff by the burden of another twenty-four months tied to the supplier. My supplier was lucky that

I was gardening at the time, which always puts me in a good mood, otherwise I may have decided to switch suppliers, as it was obvious that she didn't care about me or my needs. In fact, at one point in her ramblings I did ask her if she could downgrade my existing package as I now realized how little of it we actually used. Had she been really interested in me as a consumer I could have told her about my new interest in football, and my family's love of drama. If she had found the right time to talk to me, and then connected deeply, there is a chance she may have been able to add value to my life with an enhanced package – and make a sale herself. But we will never know. I knew she didn't care and it was enough to make me want to return to the weeding as soon as I could.

You will find that when you put your energy into discovering needs first, you do more than get information about your buyer's situation. You build the rapport that is critical in establishing the trust needed in order for the potential customer to say yes to your proposal. Every buying process requires the consumer to discover for themselves the unmet needs that will drive their decision-making. If you are there to help them, you are in the best position to sell your product or service.

Better questioning

> *I keep six honest serving men (they taught me all*
> *I knew); their names are What and Why and When,*
> *and How and Where and Who* – Rudyard Kipling

The better the questions you ask, the more likely you are to help your buyer discover something new. That is why it is so important to ask questions that open up a discussion, and stimulate the buyer's thinking. This is also why the 'open questions' that taught Kipling so much are a critical tool in the sales process. Your ability to master them will increase your likelihood of being a great salesperson. It amazes me how, in workshops, people nod knowingly when I introduce this subject, and then fail to apply the ideas in practice. What is an 'open question'? An open question is one that is framed to demand more than a yes or no answer. Often salespeople, despite knowing about open questions, fail to use them because they slip into the assumptive mode. All they want to discover is whether the person in front of them agrees with what they already know. This kind of assumptive questioning fails to help us understand needs and build rapport.

TRY THIS NOW: Think of a potential customer and write a list of ten questions that will help you to discover their needs. Look back at your list. How many of them were 'open' (starting with 'who', 'what', 'where', 'when', 'how' or 'why')? Reframe the 'closed' questions you asked so that they now can't be answered as simply yes or no. Notice your tendency to frame questions as 'closed', and think of a way to remind yourself, when you are preparing for meetings, of the importance of keeping your questioning – and your mind – open.

The challenge with closed questions

Closed questions are not bad in themselves, but they do present a challenge at this stage of the sales process. They can sound interrogational, and unless the potential customer is already in deep rapport with you, or really wants to talk, they get little in response. Importantly, they direct the mind of the listener down a fixed path, so they don't encourage an exploration of the situation. I must stress here that your attitude and intention are more important than simply the words you use. Research highlighted in Neil Rackham's book *SPIN Selling* indicates that the obsession of sales trainers with encouraging open questions doesn't always stack up. Rackham suggests that results depend on the kind of questions you ask.[8] That said, my experience is that reframing questions as 'open' is a critical step to encouraging more radiant thinking in buyers. If you have a deep rapport with someone and they clearly want to talk, then the linguistic structure of the questions you ask won't matter. In situations where you are less known and trusted, the framing of the question is critical.

Deeper probing using Socratic questioning

As our intention is to dig deeper, there is a useful tool that many influencers use intuitively. What you instinctively do when you are really interested is to ask questions that naturally follow from the answer you were given. This form of questioning was popularized by the Greek philosopher Socrates, who said, 'Let the answer be the mother of the next question.'

In practice, this means framing your next question with words from the answer you have just heard. Let's imagine we are watching Socrates use this type of questioning on a pupil in Ancient Greece. As I haven't ever been to Ancient Greece, we replicated this in my kitchen with my seven-year-old daughter, Saffron – who was quite bemused when I appeared wearing a bedroom sheet to get into role.

Socrates: 'Saffron, what is the meaning of life?'

Saffron: 'Gymnastics?'

Socrates: 'And why, for you, do you think that *gymnastics* adds meaning to life?'

Saffron: 'I just love learning new moves and the feeling I get when I can finally do it.'

Socrates: 'And why do you think *learning new moves* is so important?'

Saffron: 'Because when I am learning new things I am stretching myself and it feels better to spend my time becoming better than I was yesterday than watching TV.'

Socrates: 'So would you say that for you the meaning of life is about *stretching yourself* to learn new things?'

Saffron: 'Yes. If you say so, Dad.'

This technique has two advantages in the sales process. Firstly, we don't have to think about the next question until the other person has completely finished speaking. Secondly, we are giving across a powerful signal that we are listening when we repeat what the other person has said. When used effectively, Socratic questioning (sometimes branded as 'linear probing' in sales training) helps us to uncover needs that we would never find by asking single questions alone. This is because what we are trying to discover is often unknown to the person we are speaking to.

One warning on using Socratic questioning: any technique in the wrong hands can be unhelpful. I was once called by a sales manager whose staff had recently been through training and had learnt this technique. She had observed one of them using it in a meeting with a university dean that went wrong. Caught in the headlights of her thinking, and with a limited understanding of the market or product, the salesperson had blindly continued to ask question after question, always following on from the last, but never getting anywhere. In order to help the buyer discover their unmet needs, you must allow time to genuinely explore what is important.

Using closed questions effectively

While closed questions do not help in gaining deeper understanding, they are helpful in confirming what we know, in clarifying our understanding and in building patterns of agreement in the sales process. It is important therefore that throughout the process of discovering needs we are constantly checking in with our buyer to ensure we are on the same page and that we understand where they are coming from.

Better listening

My old sales director, Karen Stacey, told me that 'You have two ears and one mouth for a reason.' She knew that great salespeople always used their ears more than their mouth. The challenge is that our ability to listen is limited and hugely impacted by the interruption of our thoughts. It seems that our ability to think as well as listen is a double-edged sword. In live training, it is easy to demonstrate the impact thinking has on listening. When I ask the simplest questions in a listening test after firing off certain mental triggers, participants fail to hear, or remember, what is being said. Neurologists are now able to track our brain chemistry, and find that when hearing involves too much internal processing, listening cannot occur. In social situations, we don't hear what's being said because we are mentally rehearsing how we are going to reply. In client meetings you might be thinking so hard about the next question, or about what you are going to say, that you fail to listen to the customer. Improving your listening skills doesn't only enable deeper discovery, it is a critical tool in establishing deeper rapport.

Listening Ladder

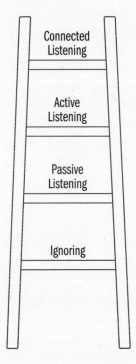

It is useful to imagine the act of listening as on a scale in which passive listening, or simply hearing, is at the bottom. We can all hear without listening, and this is the kind of listening that we will use if we are disinterested, or disengaged. When we are given complex data to process, thinking of something else or distracted in any way, we are hearing rather than listening. That said, we can engineer our environment and structure our meetings and phone calls so as to avoid distractions, and maximize our ability to listen. Knowing that we may be distracted by thought is a useful tool in itself. As you increase your awareness of these barriers to listening, you will find yourself more able to get back in the moment, and shift to a state of active – or even connected – listening.

TRY THIS NOW: The key barriers to listening are listed below. Note how and when your listening is compromised by any one of them.

— Thinking of what to say
— Thinking of the next question
— Reacting to what has been said (to agree or disagree)
— The need to warm up (our brain sometimes misses the first part of a sentence)
— Complex data (once we start processing it, we compromise our listening)
— Physical distractions
— Mental distractions (stray thoughts)

Take a moment to notice the impact of these barriers on your ability to connect with others. Notice how when you are agitated or in a low mood, your listening may be even more affected by the barriers you have noted.

Now reflect on what you may be able to do – either physically or mentally – to avoid being impacted in this way. How can you set up your meetings or phone calls to ensure your capacity to listen with empathy? Bear in mind that the impact is often simply in the noticing. When we register the role played by thought in our listening we can instantly reconnect.

Active listening

I've spent much of my life as a sales trainer encouraging people to listen 'actively'. Observing the behaviour of those who build rapport naturally and effectively, we see that there are certain clues that tell us they are listening. They may tilt their head slightly, nod, make encouraging noises, ask follow-up questions, or even lean towards the person they are listening to. For many, simply copying these active signs of listening automatically improves our concentration, and our ability to focus on the other person. This is what we mean by 'active' listening. Accompanied by clarifying questions, and a genuine interest in discovery, this can be a useful strategy to improve your listening skills. Taking notes, asking questions to confirm what you have heard, and careful recapping will also help you to listen more effectively. This is not, however, the most impactful and effective kind of listening.

Connected listening

You may have experienced a moment in your life when you connected so deeply with another person that you could tangibly feel they were unequivocally listening. Rather than listening in order to make a point, they were listening in a way that went beyond reasoning. They were listening with a complete attention that meant they were without their own thoughts for a moment. They were completely connected to you.

This is what I call 'connected listening'. Connected listening is when there is nothing beyond the listening. And when this occurs we feel so supported that we are able to move beyond our current level of thinking into a different area of consciousness. This is why connected listening is the foundation of therapy and counselling. Simply being heard in this way is enough for many to see their own wisdom, and to discover what they didn't know they knew. Which is why it is such a useful tool in a sales process. If your customer can experience connected listening, they can discover and share previously unknown truths about their situation.

Building rapport through questioning

Recently I watched a friend of mine being chatted up in a bar, and after twenty minutes of talking to this attractive stranger, I asked her a little about him. Surprisingly, she knew nothing, but was nonetheless convinced that he was 'really nice'! It is worth noting what happened there in relation to the value of good questioning and listening in the sales process. As Dr Robert Cialdini makes clear in his book *Pre-Suasion*, it is the stuff that happens *before we ask* that has the greatest impact on someone's likelihood of saying yes.[9] In the example of my friend at the bar, the process of good listening and good questioning created a sense of 'liking' that is proven by behavioural science, and our own intuition as buyers and sellers, to increase sales results. People like to be heard, and if you provide your customers with the opportunity to be heard during the sales process, you will increase rapport and thus your chances of a sale.

The questioning funnel

A useful model I use with many sales teams is the 'questioning funnel'. This is an approach to questioning that starts with the big picture and then gradually narrows down to discussion of specific organizational and personal needs. The idea is that it is often easier to start by talking about things a little further away from the immediate issues. We therefore get to build our conversation and understanding by seeing the wider context of what we need to cover. In preparing for a sales meeting it is therefore useful to think of some 'big picture questions' that can start the ball rolling, and then some questions that begin to narrow the focus a little towards the areas you are likely to be able to support. What you see below is a framework that can apply to many organizations. You may want to adjust it to your own specific needs and attach some key questions that will help you to find areas to discuss when you are face to face with a customer. Remember: not every meeting needs to cover all these areas, but an understanding of them will help a seller offer real value in both their questioning and their proposition.

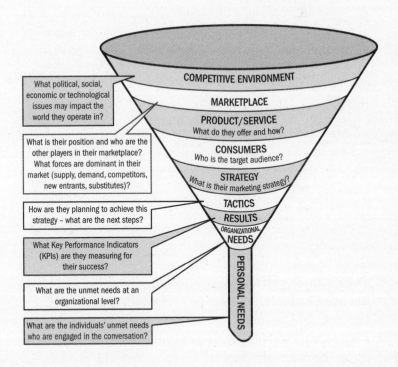

TRY THIS NOW

1. Create a questioning funnel framework – Looking at the example framework above, create a framework for your own customer base that will be helpful in customer meetings. What areas after Environment and Marketplace will you want to cover to get a deeper understanding of the world your customers live in? Create, in your notebook, a questioning funnel framework that lists at least four levels you can explore before you reach organizational and personal needs. To be clear: you will not always have to make discoveries based on all these levels. It is only a framework to help you and your customer explore the bigger picture before getting into the specifics of the issues.

2. Create some model questions – For each level of your funnel, list two or three questions you could ask that may help the customer to communicate and discover for themselves something about their needs as an organization or an individual. Make sure the questions are open in their structure, and you are confident that they will be helpful in building your understanding of your customers' needs.

Closing the discovering needs phase effectively

I'm often asked how long the discovering needs phase should be. Like a piece of string, there is no defined length, but only a defined intention. The process is finished when you are clear that you have discovered the unmet needs that you can satisfy. And that's it.

So what happens if you haven't uncovered any unmet needs? Well, technically the process is finished. If selling is the matching of unmet needs with a product or service, then without unmet needs there can be no sale. That's the truth. It is better at this stage to walk away without presenting anything than to present your proposition. In the photo-copier business we were taught that this situation warranted use of the 'business card close'. We were told if we couldn't find a need, we should hand the customer a business card and say something like, 'Thanks for your time. As you don't really see any need for what we are offering I won't waste any of your time by presenting to you, but if you do ever find yourself in a position where you see a need, then please do contact me.' It is a brave person who leaves a meeting without presenting their proposition, but bearing in mind that so many presentations never lead to a sale, it is the right thing to do.

Once the need is defined, however, there are a few things that can help you move the sale forward. The first is to get a confirmation that you really understand the need. The second is to make sure that you haven't missed anything, and the last is to get some kind of agreement that, in principle, it is worth you moving forward to make a proposal. These three steps help you enter the next stage of the sale with clarity and a commitment towards making a decision.

Confirming the need should be easy if you have defined it well to begin with. You just need to ensure you are agreed on the language you are using, and that the need is clear.

The second move is really useful and for this reason is

sometimes called the 'safety net'. It's a simple question: 'Is there anything else I need to know?' This ensures that nothing has been missed. While it sounds obvious, it often yields information and revelations that are far from obvious. A coach of mine recently used it in a business meeting and discovered that their key competition had been ruled out of the running. I used it quite recently to discover that my key contact was about to leave the business. Don't forget to use it yourself to find out what you may have missed.

You should know that I agonized over whether to include this final stage in this book, because I use it so rarely nowadays. My experience is that if you have defined the need well enough and are clearly confirming this need all the way along, you don't really require an expressed intention to buy at this stage. That said, many people swear by it, so I am presenting it to you as an option, rather than a definitive tool. The 'conditional close' is effective for some because it asks a question of the buyer that creates a pre-agreement. In situations where you go to some lengths to create a proposal for them, it will be absolutely necessary to do this. In essence it is a simple question: 'If I can show you that our product or service matches your needs . . . will you buy it?'

In practice you can amend this to suit your situation. If I am going to create a proposal that will require time, then I will still say something to the effect of, 'If I put together a proposal for you to share in the business that shows how we will utilize the training days, will you be able to secure the budget to make it happen?'

The advantage of doing this is that you get to really see at this point whether the person is in a position to buy your product or service. The answer is rarely a straightforward yes, but the discussion that follows will prepare you for the process that you will need to go through to win the sale. They may say, 'Yes, but I'll need to talk to X', or 'Yes, but we will also need to go through procurement', or 'Yes, but I am seeing three other suppliers so it will depend on their proposals too'. The important part is that by asking the question you not only express your confidence in your solution, but you also get to determine what barriers may be in the way of making it happen.

CHECKLIST

— Are you genuinely interested in finding out more about the person or business you are seeking to sell to?

— Have you mastered your use of 'open questions', so you naturally ask questions that expand your customer's thinking?

— Are you confirming throughout the discussions that you really understand their needs?

— Are you using Socratic questioning – using the answers from customers' questions to discover more about their needs and motivations?

— What level are you habitually listening at? Are you simply hearing, actively listening or engaging in 'connected listening'?

— What can you do to improve the level of listening you employ in important areas of your life?

— How can you use the idea of your questioning funnel to prepare questions that move from the big picture down to more strategic and tactical understanding of customer needs?

— Are you using a 'safety net' to make sure you haven't missed anything?

— Do you get clear confirmation of your customer's needs before you move on to present your solution?

— Is there a 'conditional close' you can use to build commitment to moving forward?

5:

MATCHING NEEDS

Never sell a product, sell the idea behind the product
– Heinz Goldman

If you jumped straight to this chapter because you want to know how to present your sales proposition, then *step away from the book*. Without a solid foundation, no one can present a coherent sales argument. In my experience, 'telling not selling' irritates customers and requires a high volume of 'no's for every 'yes'. It's an appropriate strategy if you are selling stuff people don't need, but if that's the case, then this chapter won't help you anyway. Only once you have found the right customer, connected with them authentically, and discovered with them what they really need, are you ready to present.

Now is the time to get your thinking hat on, and present a targeted case for meeting those needs. This is how you raise desire.

To understand how to do this we can look at the strategies used by the world's best advertising agencies. While marketing is becoming more complex, the fundamentals remain the same: advertisers seek to demonstrate through their advertising the benefit the consumer will get from using their products. Occasionally you will see them doing different stuff, but in the main, advertising aims to show what the product will do *for you*, rather than what the product *is*. This principle is critical, because when we understand it we get to see how we should present any product or service in a way that is most appealing to its consumer.

Look at the majority of car advertising. A sector that needs to spend huge amounts across TV, press, outdoor and online to keep their products occupying the right place in their consumers' minds. Rarely today will you see a car ad that shows very much of the car. What you will see is a description of the experiences and feelings that you will unlock if you become an owner of one of these dream machines. Cars targeting young people will promise them freedom from their parents, cars targeting young men will promise them women, and cars targeting families will promise them happy kids and a balanced home life. Fashion advertising promises us sex appeal and community, fragrance ads promise us self-esteem and sex appeal, and ice cream and Diet Coke ads promise us more sex. Of course, none of these products really deliver on these promises, but they attempt to tap into the unfulfilled needs of their consumers, and demonstrate how the product will meet these needs.

Benefits sell

An important word in all of this is 'benefits'. People buy when they are convinced that a product will benefit them personally.

So what is a benefit? A benefit is something that brings a positive change to your situation. Largely we experience benefits as financial or geared towards our convenience and comfort. If you can demonstrate that a product will save money, save time, or make someone feel good, it is likely to sell. Products and services produce real benefits when they can be seen to match needs. The personalization of these benefits is largely what the 'active' part of the sales process is all about.

David Ogilvy, the father of modern advertising, knew this well. Prior to becoming a copywriter, Ogilvy had been in sales himself and wrote a manual in the late 1950s that included some of the advice contained in this book today. He knew the power of benefits and he rocked his client, and the agency he worked in, when he first presented the now famous advertising for the new Rolls Royce Silver Shadow in the 1970s. Instead of the normal list of features, Ogilvy focused on a seemingly random benefit. The headline read *At 70 mph, you can still hear the clock ticking* and there was a picture of the luxurious dashboard in view.

His colleagues were bemused. Where was the usual list of product features? Ogilvy had to fight to present the idea to the client. He won the argument, and it proved to be the most effective advertising Rolls Royce had ever run.

FABs: Distinguishing Features, Advantages and Benefits

Ogilvy would say, 'Sell the sizzle, not the sausage.'[10]

The best way to sell a product is not to focus on the cold hard facts, but to use those facts to highlight what the product really means to the customer. To do this, let me introduce the concept of FABs (Features, Advantages and Benefits). Understanding the difference between them, and presenting your sales points as a series of FABs will help your customer to appreciate how your product meets their needs, and will therefore raise their desire to buy.

Feature – Single indisputable fact about the product.

Advantage – Why that fact is notable, or what is good about that feature.

Benefit – How that feature benefits the customer.

During sales training, the only distinction many people make is between features and benefits. This misses out the advantage step and sometimes means the benefit isn't clear. The benefit is personal. Emotional. Tailored to the individual you are speaking to. Distinguishing between the three enables you to connect the *fact of the feature* to the *generic advantage of that feature*, and thus to the personal benefit that it brings the customer.

TRY THIS NOW

1. Distinguishing FABs – Explore this concept by taking a product you own and separating a single feature from its advantage and its benefit. For example, let's choose a pen:

— *Feature:* Retractable nib.

— *Advantage:* Enables you to store it without potentially marking other items.

— *Benefit:* Stops you getting marks on your clothes or furnishings.

Do this now for a product you own, and then do the same for a product or service that you sell. Pick out three different features that you would normally high-light to customers. See if you can distinguish the advantage and the benefit of that particular feature and write it down in your notebook as a FAB.

2. Applying the 'so what?' test – Once you have done it, ask yourself 'so what?' By asking this a few times, it is amazing how much further we can go to distinguishing a benefit.

What happens when we ask 'so what?' about the pen with the retractable nib?

It would stop you from ruining your bag.
'So what?'
Pens can mark your bag and the things you have in it.
'So what?'
It would save you having to buy a new bag.
'So what?'
It would save you the hassle and money.

There's the benefit. You can always make the benefit clearer if you ask yourself 'so what?' a few times. Try this now with one of the examples you created in step 1.

Linking the benefit to unmet needs

In the previous chapter we focused not only on uncovering unmet needs, but on clarifying them with the potential buyer and confirming that these needs were important to them. It is important to bring these needs to the front of your customers' minds before you present anything about the features (or benefits) of the product. We call this a 'hook'. It is something that grabs someone's attention, by highlighting what he or she has already said about an unmet need.

It could sound something like this:

'Remember you told me earlier that you were struggling to keep up with the paperwork?'

It's a simple reminder that has the effect of raising the customer's awareness of a need, just before you present the solution. It's important because our listening is sometimes compromised (Chapter 4, see page 56).

The idea is that you use the hook before you present the FAB, and then you follow this with a question that asks the customer to confirm if the feature mentioned does actually meet their need. If you have matched a feature with a need, then it will be easy to get active agreement from your customer and begin the process of moving towards a sale.

As you are likely to have discussed a number of needs and your product will have many features, it is worth carefully considering how you can present, one by one, the key features of your product or service. Presenting any feature in isolation of an unmet need is likely to backfire, eliciting an unexpressed 'so what?'

Let me give you some examples. You know how you picked up this book because you wanted to achieve more sales (hook)? A FAB is a simple tool that can enable a salesperson to point to the benefit a product will bring by distinguishing between the facts, the generic advantages and the benefit (feature). Fabs enable a salesperson to get more traction because they engage the customer on a journey from fact to a personal realization of how that relates to them (advantage). They will help you get more sales because you will be able to link your product directly to the customer's need, and by showing the link you'll raise desire (benefit). Can you see how they will help you increase your sales (agreement)?

This stage of the sale is called matching. Reaching agreement at every point along the way is important for you because it tells you whether your customer really sees the connection.

Making your sales points more attractive

If you speak to a person in language he knows,
it goes to his head. If you speak to him in his own
language, it goes to his heart
– Nelson Mandela

I am often asked for tips on how to make sales presentations more attractive, or what language to use in order to make arguments more appealing. The truth is, I don't know. Without being present myself, it is impossible to tell. So my only advice is for you to be there 100 per cent, to pay attention to what is in front of you and to speak about your product or service factually *and* from the heart.

That said, the quote above from Nelson Mandela reveals an important truth about selling, although it was evidently not the point he intended to make. You need to adapt your pitch to the style and language that appeals to the customer. There is no silver bullet sales line that will cut through every person. Paying careful attention to the style and language of your customer enables you to tailor your approach.

In neuro-linguistic programming studies, scientists found

that great influencers always adapt their language in order to take account of how people process information in their brains. The suggestion is that more 'visual' people respond better to pictures, more 'auditory' people to sound, and more 'kinaesthetic' people to feelings. Taught in the classroom, this theory makes sense, but when I have observed people trying to apply the technique, they get too stuck in their own thinking for it to have much effect. That said, if you do notice that the person you are speaking to has a tendency towards any of these traits, you can automatically make an adjustment in your presentation style. Especially if you are able to sufficiently step away from your thinking to connect to the person you are talking to. More about that in Chapter 8.

USPs: Unique selling points

Marketeers across the world have an obsession with USPs, or 'unique selling points'. These are features of a product (or service) that are unique to that product (or service), and also of value to the customer. It's a useful distinction and worth exploring. This is because if you understand your product's USPs, you can position them in your sales presentations to eliminate competition. The challenge is that in today's world they are hard to find, and easy to imitate.

So what really is a USP? Well, we all know what the word 'unique' means – it's something that is a one-off, and in business it is something that your competitors don't have. A selling point is less easily defined. A USP is therefore something really unique that genuinely adds value to customers, and that they are prepared to pay for. When you explore the concept in depth you will see that there are many very successful products that don't really have USPs. This is useful to know because these kinds of offerings need to market differently, and require a more emotional or brand-based approach (e.g. Coca-Cola).

> **TRY THIS NOW:** Looking at the product or service you are selling, see if you can list the top three features that can be described as USPs. Are they truly unique? Do none of your competitors have the same feature? Do these features genuinely add value to your customers? Be honest with yourself here. It's OK not to have many, or any, USPs. It's useful, however, to know.

Using USPs wisely

If you are confident that you have USPs that add value, then you should position them carefully when making a sales presentation. You should be aware of what behavioural scientists call the 'primacy effect' and the 'recency effect', which suggest that the first and the last things heard in an argument are most likely to be remembered. Placing your focus on what you consider to be really unique will help ensure that your most powerful sales points are remembered and therefore play a positive role in your customer's decision-making.

If you can't think of any USPs, then you will need to work harder if you are in a competitive market. While your relationship will sometimes be enough to tip the balance, you may want to consider whether you can make some kind of adjustment to your package or service that can enable it to be positioned as unique. When I was working with a large training company we created our own unique learning evaluation system to position ourselves as unique. Now everyone has a similar system available via the web. This same company now writes their own books, that aren't available via Amazon, in order to create a USP for their otherwise indistinguishable training offerings. The interesting thing is that the evaluation system or the books didn't really need to be of any kind of quality to produce a perceivable USP in the mind of the customer. My suggestion would be to do your best to try and find useful USPs that really do add value. That way you won't only be able to make sales today, but you will find it much easier to make sales tomorrow.

The last point is important. Making sales based on promised USPs that don't actually benefit the customer is a fool's game. It requires effort to get a new customer. If the promise they are buying into isn't real, they will feel disappointed and you'll be working harder next year to make more sales. Since I set up on my own – and stopped making promises I couldn't deliver – my life has become so much easier. When you are selling, if you take care to ensure that the benefits you are presenting are real, and the features deliverable, you can make your life easier too.

CHECKLIST

— Have you clearly defined the customer's unmet needs?

— Do you understand which features you have to sell, and what advantages and benefits they bring?

— Are you able to use a 'hook' before presenting each

feature, to ensure the customer is connected in the moment to their unmet needs?

— Will you always ensure that after every FAB you get a clear agreement from the customer that the feature matches their need?

— Do you understand which of your features really are USPs?

— Can you prepare to present your USPs in a way that has most effect?

— Are you tailoring the language and feel of your presentation to the individual person and organization?

6:
AGREEMENT

If you watch any influencer at work, there is an easy way to tell if they are getting through. Look at the head of the person they are speaking to. You will see it nod. Either consciously or unconsciously, a person who persuades manages to create a pattern of agreement in the person they are speaking to that causes them to nod, murmur or yell. Preachers in church will shout, 'Can I get a witness?' Lawyers in court will lean in to the jury and ask, 'Do you see what this means?' Children will nod at their parents and ask, 'Again?' If you want to influence a sales process, you will benefit from understanding the importance of creating patterns of agreement.

While agreement requires a chapter in its own right, in truth it is not a stage in the sales process at all. It is something that will permeate every step of a sale. It demands its own chapter because of its importance in the process, and because reflection and decision have their own stages in the buying process. This is because after a person has been presented with a sales proposition the natural thing to do is to question it and check whether they agree. That person's tendency won't be to agree automatically and, particularly if it is a big decision, he/she will pose some objections, and look at the alternatives to 'yes'.

In this chapter, I will show you how the most effortless persuaders use a staircase of agreement throughout their sales process. This takes advantage of the human tendency towards being consistent. We will also explore some classic techniques to overcome common objections, which will enable you to confidently deal with your customer's natural tendency to question, and prevent you from becoming defensive or pushy.

Professor Robert Cialdini, in his leading book *Influence*, suggested that over and above good reason there are certain triggers that predispose humans towards saying 'yes'.[11] That is, while we may think we are buying a product or service to meet an unmet need, or to provide a benefit, our decision-making is swayed by a number of other factors. You know that you are more likely to buy from someone you like, so the principle of liking should be no surprise to you. You will also know that humans are social animals so you will be able to accept that 'social proof' is a powerful trigger towards agreement. Cialdini also suggests that authority, reciprocation, scarcity and consistency are universal human triggers that predispose us to acceptance.

Consistency is the tool that is most critical throughout the sales process, and central to getting agreement. Human beings are consistency-driven animals: we value consistency highly and we will do a lot to prove we are consistent. Consider this: if I met you and told a friend that I liked you but did think you were inconsistent, I suspect you wouldn't be too happy with my analysis. It seems that something is hardwired in human conditioning to make us want to be consistent. This becomes a useful tool for anyone trying to sell anything. If you can demonstrate that the decision is consistent with previous decisions, it is easier to get a 'yes'. If a proposition feels like it requires a person to make a choice that is inconsistent, it is a harder argument to make.

> **TRY THIS NOW:** Think about the product or service you are selling. In what ways is it similar to a product or service that customers have already bought? List a number of things you can mention throughout the sales conversation that will remind them of the consistency of their approach.

Cialdini's work also explains why once we have bought something small in a store, it is easy for us to continue spending. Once we have made a commitment we are ready to expand on it, because it is consistent with the decision we already made. The research is fascinating. People who have agreed to do the smallest things, like placing a sticker in their window, are three times more likely to accept a much larger request, like positioning a huge poster on their lawn. Anyone who has spent time shopping may appreciate this phenomenon: once we start buying, it's harder to stop.

The agreement staircase

Recently I was disturbed by a call on my mobile as I was enjoying a stroll in the park. As it was an international number I suspected it was an associate, so I answered the call. The call went something like this:

Me: 'Hello.'

Caller: 'Hello, this is Charles calling from ITC Communications. Is that Mr Presman?'

Me: 'Yes.'

Caller: 'Mr Presman, do you have a mobile phone?'

Me: 'Yes.' (Ignoring the fact that this was obvious as he had called me on it.)

Caller: 'Mr Presman, do you spend more than £10.50 a month on your mobile communication billing?'

Me: 'Yes.' (Even though I could see where this was going, wanted none of it, and was beginning to feel manipulated.)

Caller: 'Mr Presman, would you like to save money on your mobile communication expenses?'

Me: 'No.'

You see, I knew that if I had said yes, I would have found it very hard to say no to the next question, which would have been something like: 'Would you like to hear how I can save you money?' Or: 'If I can save you money, will you change your contract with me today?'

While this was a crude usage, it was a demonstration of what is called 'the agreement staircase'. This concept is central to most sales approaches, and involves gaining consistent agreement from the customer throughout the process. Pushy salespeople often use this rather crudely to try and force you into agreement, but when used more

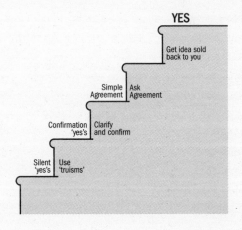

subtly it can have a positive effect. Because we don't like to be inconsistent, if we are consistently agreeing with someone throughout a conversation we will find it difficult to disagree with him or her at the end of it. Especially if they have built a logical argument based on what we have said, and on our genuine needs.

There are a number of ways to get this agreement and each of them helps build a pattern.

1. Truisms

At the most subtle level, we can use language patterns that create internal agreement. Politicians, preachers and hypnotists use these patterns all the time. I first learnt about them from studying the UK's leading hypnotist, Paul McKenna. When I saw him on stage it was immediately clear that he was using some more obvious tools to get agreement. He was repeating people's answers, nodding and returning answers as questions in order to get his subjects to say yes.

Paul McKenna (in response to an answer): 'Ah, so you work in publishing?'

Subject: 'Yes.'

Paul McKenna: 'So do you work for a publisher?'

Subject: 'Yes.'

Paul McKenna: 'Who do you work for?'

Subject: 'Macmillan.'

Paul McKenna: 'Oh, they are quite big in the world of books, aren't they?'

Subject: 'Yes.'

Paul McKenna: 'They have lots of different publishing houses, don't they?'

Subject: 'Yes.'

Yet that wasn't the most interesting tool he was using to get agreement. It seemed that he was saying things that were deliberately designed to get them to *think* 'yes'.

Paul Kenna: 'So, I imagine that as you have been waiting you may have been wondering what I am going to say to you and you may also have been wondering what I might ask you to do and how much you will be able to go into a trance today.'

Now if you were about to be hypnotized by Paul McKenna, I'm sure you would have been thinking those things too. What he had done was to say some things that would automatically elicit a silent yes.

He was using a technique that I subsequently discovered was commonly used in hypnosis: the use of an obvious statement to build a pattern of agreement in the subject's mind. This tool is not only used by hypnotists, but also employed by politicians and their speechwriters. It helps to build confidence in the mind of the listener. To quote from one of my father's political speeches from the late 1970s:

'We don't mine cabbages. You can't give cornflakes for Christmas. We all want a government that treats people fairly.'

You can see why my father didn't win his by-election with lines like that, but repeating something that is true is a simple way to build agreement.

TRY THIS NOW: Think of some truisms that you could use when you are speaking to customers. Write them down and check that they are likely to elicit a yes without sounding too blindingly obvious.

2. Confirmation

The next level of agreement is simple confirmation. This is where you repeat information that you have already gained to both check your understanding and build patterns of agreement. You can do this throughout the sales process. If you are doing it solely to get the person to say yes, it will be irritating – as in the example of the phone salesman (see page 80). If you use it carefully, though, it will give you an opportunity to check your understanding and build agreement. You can achieve this kind of agreement through confirming what you already know, or confirming what you are learning throughout the conversation.

During any sales conversation there are so many opportunities to get this kind of simple yes.

3. Simple agreement

In Chapter 5, we discussed presenting a sales point, and you learnt that after every FAB should come a question to elicit agreement (see page 72). This kind of agreement is powerful because it compels the customer to agree with the argument you are making. Once they are in agreement that each feature you present matches one of their needs, the principle of consistency begins to tie them into accepting your solution.

There are other opportunities, however, to elicit agreement of this type. When you are asking questions to confirm the need, you might ask whether they agree that this is an important issue. If you remain really interested in the other person, you will naturally be asking this kind of question in order to check whether you are aligned in your thinking.

4. Complex agreement

To take full advantage of the principle of commitment, you need to get your customer to repeat back to you the argument you are making, in his or her own words. This form of agreement is very powerful because once a customer has articulated the sales proposition themselves, he or she is unlikely to disagree with it.

Prior to this we have been looking for a yes, so we have been using closed questions. Now we use an open question to ask the customer to consider how the proposal will meet their needs, for example:

'How will this work in your business?'

'What benefit can you see this having on your staff?'

'How convinced are you that this will answer the issues you are concerned about?'

This kind of questioning does two important things. It tests the effectiveness of your sales pitch, and it gives the customer the opportunity to check whether he or she can see the benefits for themselves. Using open questions in this way is a very effective method of eliciting an agreement, meaning that you are ready to close the sale.

5. Non-verbal agreement

You don't just want to hear 'yes', you are looking to see physical signs of agreement as well. To encourage this, you will also need to make the right signs yourself. Nodding will help the customer align with what you are saying, and test whether you are in agreement. Try it next time you are making a proposition.

Overcoming customer objections

It is rare that I meet a sales manager who doesn't want me to help his salespeople overcome customer objections. This is because when sales fail and prospective buyers are asked for reasons why they didn't agree to the sale, they come up with the most interesting excuses. The most common one is money. Either 'It's too expensive', or 'I don't have the money', and this is closely followed by 'I don't need it', or 'There is a better product out there'. While sometimes these objections will be true, in many cases they are simply the result of a poorly executed sales process.

I'm not suggesting that this is not what thousands of sales professionals are hearing every day. It's just that in my experience these so-called 'objections' are usually no more than smoke screens disguising something more critical. If a person engages in a sales conversation in business, they are likely to buy if they can really see a benefit. You should only engage with customers who you know are in a position to buy. What is usually going on, however, when they raise objections, is that they simply haven't seen how the product or service is going to benefit them sufficiently to warrant parting with their cash. This can be because either they haven't seen a great enough unmet need to solve, or they can't see how your product will solve the issue.

Therefore, most 'objections' are not objections at all; they are simply signals that the salesperson hasn't adequately helped the customer to appreciate an unmet need, or shown how this unmet need can be met with the proposed product or service. Personally, I would prefer to get to the point with a customer where we realize that there really isn't a need for the product that warrants the investment than end up pretending that there is a need and then failing to show that our product meets it.

In my experience, when people really don't want to buy they go so cold on you that you simply can't speak to them. If you are in a situation where they are still engaging in a conversation, then they are still in the sales process and the objection is sometimes no more than a request for more information. Telling you that the product is too expensive, or that there are features in another product that appeal to them, is often a way of asking how your product or service can work for them.

Are they factual or emotional objections?

A useful frame through which to look at objections is to see if they are being expressed in a factual or emotional way. The challenge of emotional objections, which involve expressions of feelings and subjective opinions, is that no amount of logic is likely to shift that opinion. It is therefore worth approaching objections differently.

Logical objections can be dealt with logically. You can try to understand what the objection is, and attempt to present a factual argument that changes the prospective buyer's mind. That is, if you can see an argument that seems real for you. We will deal with more emotional objections in the next section.

Don't fight objections – welcome them

The biggest mistake in handling customers' objections is to go into a combative mode. In this case your aim becomes to prove to them that they are wrong and you are right. You may win the battle, but you probably won't win the war. At this stage of the sale it is critical to stay connected and in rapport, and so we need to be sensitive and empathetic. The problem of pushing against objections is that most people will just push back, and then you'll have a fight. That's why we always teach people to genuinely welcome objections. Seriously.

What that means is that you should be positive when someone expresses an objection. If you really care, this should be natural. You want to discover what is behind the objection and whether there is anything in it that can help you to convince them.

DEBTS: Discover, Empathize, Be honest, Trial close, Solve

There are two simple formulas to help you handle objections. The DEBTS formula is an adaptation of a classic formula where I have added Be Honest into the equation. If you dig into the objection and you discover that you can't really overcome it, that there isn't anything you can say which will really change their mind, then the best thing you can do is to say so. If you end up agreeing with them, then doing anything more than empathizing and being honest will not serve you well in the long run. It may even be that after being honest they will let you know something else.

Discover – The first way of dealing with any objection is to dig deeper, connect, and ask questions. Using the same tools from the discovering needs section, you question, listen, and attempt to understand more. Only when you really understand the objection, and can fully appreciate where the other party is coming from, should you move on.

Empathize – Empathy is the understanding of someone

else's position. The objective of the discovery phase is to get empathy. You do understand, but it doesn't mean you will agree. You should be looking to express, however, before you move on, that you really appreciate where they are coming from.

Be honest – If you have no answer to their objection, be honest. Tell them it's something you've never come across, or that you have come across it before and you have no answer. Leave it open to return to at a later stage. Being honest, and asking for time to explore further, will help you stay connected with your prospect.

Trial close – If your questioning has given you a deeper understanding of the other person's position and you have discovered a rationale for them to change their mind, check first that they are willing to hear it. Ask them for permission to present your argument in the way of a trial close. Say to them:

'If I am able to change your mind, would you be interested in hearing it?'

'If I could show you an example that would demonstrate you may be wrong, would you be happy to listen?'

'If I could demonstrate a solution to your problem, would you still consider buying my product?'

This is an important stage. Having expressed an objection, and discussed it with you in detail, the reasoning may have become more ingrained. You need to check that they will listen before it is worth trying to change their mind. Sometimes when you ask this question you may find a different objection is in place.

Solve – If you have discovered a rationale for the objection, then here is an opportunity for you to present your view. Use FABs, focus on benefits, and be brief. Ensure you give an opportunity for them to agree with your case by asking for confirmation once you have presented your ideas.

Dealing with emotional objections: feel, felt, found

The classic objection-handling technique is called 'feel, felt, found'. The problem with it is that, as a formula, it sounds formulaic. If a customer feels you are using a technique on them, it can break rapport.

Before using the feel, felt, found technique you will need to do some discovery in order to appreciate what the objection is. The only way you will be able to genuinely feel what the customer is saying is if you have done this.

Feel – 'I understand how you feel.' In this stage you demonstrate your empathy, which must be real and only expressed after an exploration of what they really mean.

Felt – 'Somebody else felt this way.' This takes you into the past tense to explain that a previous customer had felt the same. The important thing is that you can only use this effectively if you have dealt with this objection before. As so many objections are common, this should be easy (if you have experience). Talk to colleagues about previous sales situations where they have successfully overcome customer objections. The only way to make this work with integrity is to use real stories with real names. Using the 'be honest' step (part of DEBTS, see page 89), and following up with colleagues with more experience, will help you build a personal database of stories to help alleviate common fears.

The power of a simple statement such as 'Mr X felt the same' is immense. It demonstrates that the customer is not alone and validates how they are feeling. It also shows that you are confident that this is a normal way for a customer to feel.

Found – 'Mr X found that when he looked into it further . . .' What you say here cannot really be scripted. You should keep the focus in the past tense and demonstrate how a different customer changed their mind and, more importantly, was therefore able to benefit in the way the current customer might also do.

CHECKLIST

— Have you confirmed what you already know, and ensured you are in agreement?

— Have you had clear agreement that there is a need to be met?

— Can you add silent agreement by using 'truisms' in your speech?

— Are you consistently checking that you are being understood, and that each of the points you make is clear?

— Are you asking the potential customer to indicate clearly if they agree that the features you are presenting match their unmet needs?

— How are you asking the customer to articulate his or her benefit?

— Are you using your whole body to help elicit agreement?

— Are you clearly questioning any objections so you really understand where the other person is coming from?

— Are you demonstrating empathy for his or her point of view?

— Can you be honest if you don't have an answer, or need time to see if there is a different way of looking at it?

— Can you determine whether the objection is factual or emotional in order to appreciate which approach may be best?

— Have you a catalogue of real customer stories you can use to deal with common objections?

— Are you prepared to use the 'trial close' to confirm whether, if you answer an objection, you will be able to agree a sale?

7:

CLOSING

This is going to be a short chapter, because closing is not as important a part of the sales process as it was once imagined to be. I don't think you'll need to learn the fifty-two closes I was taught when I sold business machines (one for each week of the year). We are beyond Always Be Closing and in the world of Attunement, Buoyancy and Clarity (Introduction, see page 7) and so closing is not the dark art it was once made out to be.

That said, if you aren't prepared at the right time to ask your customer to commit to doing business with you, it is possible you will lose sales. Have you ever been ready to buy something, and then just lost your desire? A differing priority presented itself, and the transaction was over. It's therefore important for you to be prepared, willing and able to close business as soon as you know the time is right.

Buying signals

If you are close to your customer, you will know when the time is right because you will witness their decision. In sales this is called a 'buying signal'. Much has been said in sales training about buying signals, which are the non-verbal clues that a customer is ready to buy. I have witnessed a number of occasions when a salesperson has talked me or someone else out of a sale. This is because once you are ready to make a decision, you don't need any more discussion. It is important that when you are presenting your case you understand this. You need to listen to the verbal and non-verbal language of your customer to be able to spot if they are saying 'yes'. It may be the way they are touching the product or the brochure. It may be how they are talking, or the questions they are asking. In every sales situation the action, questions and behaviours will be different, but there will be common themes for you to look out for.

Once they are ready, it is important to move on and complete the sale.

> **TRY THIS NOW:** Think about a situation in which you are selling. In order to increase your likelihood of seeing and reacting to buying signals in your customers, consider and list the following:
>
> 1. What physical actions might your customer make if they are becoming attached to your product or are ready to buy?
>
> 2. What questions might they ask if they are starting to really consider buying?

What stops us from closing?

1. Fear of rejection

What stops most people closing sales is the fear of rejection. We just don't like to hear no. Successful people don't care, however. Traditionally, this has meant that only thick-skinned, or less emotionally sensitive, people have thrived in sales environments because they didn't take rejection personally. Anyone can develop this attitude. It is a measure of emotional intelligence to be aware of your fear of rejection and to ask for something regardless. As soon as we realize that there is no link between our own emotional well-being and the customer saying yes or no, we are free to ask. Knowing that 'no' simply means that we either haven't presented an argument well enough, or that the need is not strong enough, is key. It has nothing to do with how valuable you are as an individual, or how happy you should be. This important link between feelings and thinking will be explored in the final chapter.

2. Fear of appearing pushy

The other thing that holds us back is the desire not to appear pushy, or to make the customer feel uncomfortable. If you suspect that this is holding you back, you need to get over it fast. If you have defined needs, and are clear you are offering value, you are doing the wrong thing if you fail to ask. By all means asks politely and allow the customer the opportunity to say no, but failing to ask doesn't serve anyone.

> **TRY THIS NOW:** The title of Susan Jeffers' book sums up this exercise and idea perfectly:
>
> *Feel the Fear and Do It Anyway.*
>
> The best way to conquer fear is to experience it, and see how easy it is to cope with rejection.

Jamie Smart, author and coach extraordinaire, taught me a useful exercise. It involves deliberately putting yourself into situations where you feel stupid, in order to demonstrate the mind's capacity to overcome the feeling and get back to your natural productive state.[12] Check it out for yourself.

Go into a store and ask for something that you know they don't sell. For example, I remember going into a fast food outlet and asking if I could get a haircut. They will think you are stupid, you will look embarrassed and confused, and then a few minutes later everything will be OK. If necessary, try this a few times. Notice the feelings before, during and after. Even if you are feeling bad afterwards, or days later, that too is OK. It will teach you a great lesson about where feelings come from. They never come from circumstances. But more about that in our final chapter.

In *Rejection Proof, How I Beat Fear and Became Invincible*, Jia Jiang details a series of similar experiments.[13] The bottom line is that you must practise being rejected until you no longer connect rejection to self-worth. As a salesperson you will need to get a number of rejections. Wrong time. Wrong person. Wrong price. Wrong connection. Wrong presentation. Most successful salespeople need to experience a degree of failure in order to get their order book filled.

I discovered something important early in my career, when I was selling photocopiers and fax machines. I found I had lots of prospects, or a large 'pipeline', but I wasn't getting enough orders. I was holding on to customers who wouldn't really say no, but were not saying yes either. Wanting to hold on to the opportunities, I kept them on my radar, and in my sales forecasts. Fortunately I was lazy and soon realized I was wasting my time. It was far easier to ask, as clearly as possible, whether they wanted to buy and, if not, why, and then move on. I became ruthless, but more efficient. I was wasting less of my customers' time, and less of my own time. See if you can do the same. As soon as you can, ask for the order – and if they say no, ask why. Then, if you don't think you can handle the objection, move on.

The myth of seven 'no's

Many sales systems will say you need to ask up to seven times before you will get a yes. Personally, I am not interested in that kind of approach. I would ask you to look for at least seven 'yes's (the agreement staircase we mentioned earlier, see page 80) before you ask for a final yes. Then, use your own judgement to decide if you need to go any further or move on. If you have done a good job of identifying needs and matching features to benefits, you shouldn't get too many 'no's.

Types of closes

While you don't need to continuously practise closing, or to learn a multitude of closes, it is worth having a few different ways to ask for a yes. Remember that closing is no more than a question to determine what comes next – an opportunity to discover if the buyer is ready. Take closing lightly and you will be able to easily ask customers for business. Practising regularly will enable you to overcome any fears of rejection, or of not looking good.

Any of these closes, especially the assumptive close, will fail and break rapport, unless you have beforehand clearly been through the sales process, built agreement and presented a clear match to unmet needs.

1. The direct close

'So, will you buy it?'
'Do you want me to set up the order for you?'

There are some useful ways of asking for a yes which are more subtle than the direct close examples above, yet the direct close clearly has its place in your selection of ways of asking for a yes.

2. The indirect close

'Would you like to pay by card?'
'Shall I get it ordered to come next week?'
'Would you like it in brown?'

This is a question that will determine, indirectly, if the person is saying yes. It could also be a technical question, which requires a response concerning delivery or payment.

3. The alternative close

'Would you like one or two?'
'Shall I arrange delivery, or will you collect?'

This is providing a couple of options, both of which will mean a yes.

4. The assumptive close

'I look forward to getting this made for you.'
'I will organize delivery now.'

This is a statement that the buyer would have to disagree with in order to say no.

5. Trial close

'If I can get it delivered next week, will you order today?'
'If I can find one in black for you, will you buy it?'

This final close is useful if you are being asked for a discount, or if there is a final technical issue you need to solve such as a delivery date. It enables you to get a yes conditional on doing something, and will allow you to test whether, if you take that extra step, your customer will confirm.

TRY THIS NOW: Thinking of a real sales situation, write out examples of how you would ask for a yes in the five ways described above.

Imagine yourself in front of a real customer and try each of the closes out loud. Notice how they sound to you. Make some adjustments to the wording so you feel more comfortable.

See if you can find opportunities to use the different kinds of closes in real situations in order to see how they sound and feel.

CHECKLIST

— Are you convinced that your customer has a real and present need that can be met with your product or service?

— Are you committed to them having this need met?

— Do you care more about their unmet need, or your unmet needs?

— Are you afraid of the customer saying no? If so, are you perhaps making this sale mean more than it should?

— Have you explored what may be holding the sale back, as in what objections your customer may or does have?

— Can you distinguish whether the objections you face are logical/rational or emotional?

— Can you find an example of someone who in the past had a similar objection that you can use as a case study of real value?

— Have you noticed enough buying signals, either through statements, questions, or non-verbal clues, to assure you the customer is ready to say yes?

8:

UNDERSTANDING PERSONALITY TO ADAPT AND CONNECT MORE EFFECTIVELY

As discussed, selling demands human connection. To best connect with another person it is important to see them as an individual and to look at how their own unique personality may impact on the way they interact with you. In this chapter I will show how understanding personality traits will help you connect more effectively. You will see how great influencers are able to adapt to and connect with others, and how an understanding of the specifics of personality will enable you to flex your own style more effectively, and therefore adapt and connect with others when you are selling.

I was first introduced to the idea of the four personality types in a sales course with Capital Radio back in the 1980s. The programme suggested that the personality of your buyer – whether you were dealing with an Expressive buyer, a Driving buyer, an Amiable buyer or an Analytical buyer – should impact the way you approached the sale. We were also taught that we should watch for our own style as well as the style of whom we were selling to. At a basic level we saw that understanding the four sales styles, which we will refer to later as 'the four colours', enables us to see which style you and your partner use most readily, and in doing so helps you to understand which parts of your personality you need to tone down or tune up in order to connect most effectively with the other party.

The four basic sales styles

Driving (Commanding Red) – This person is more outcome-focused in his or her approach.

Expressive (Inspiring Yellow) – This person is more sociable, idea-focused and flexible.

Amiable (Empowering Green) – This person is more people-focused, adaptable and gentle.

Analytical (Conscientious Blue) – This person is more practical, detail-focused and reflective.

Knowing which of the above sales styles best describes you and your buyer is a useful tool to help you adapt to and connect with the different people you need to influence.

I was soon able to see that by noticing how my style contrasted with or complemented that of my buyer, I could adapt to and connect with them more effectively. It became clear that different sales styles have their own ways of behaving during the sales process. For example, Expressives (Inspiring Yellows) like to jump in quickly and be spontaneous. They enjoy the flexible approach and the interaction that comes with buying without too much preparation. However, Analytical buyers (Conscientious Blues) prefer a more structured approach and value order and process. I remember realizing that one of my main contacts was much more 'Analytical' than me. The realization was enough to cause me to tone down my more 'Expressive' elements and include some more process-driven variables to move our relationship forward. Having once found them a 'difficult' person to deal with, I was soon connecting well with this customer. Therefore, as a salesperson, it is useful to be able to understand and measure personality in some way.

The roots of psychometrics (the measurement of aspects of a person's personality) stretch back more than 2,500 years, to when Hippocrates put forth the idea of the four humours: the elements that linked to human health. This system divided people up into four types: phlegmatics, melancholics, sanguines and cholerics. These four types closely resemble the modern theories of personality archetypes.

The model of personality classification we're looking at in this chapter is called Lumina Spark. It builds on a long history of personality classification, from Hippocrates through to Jung's eight personality types in the early twentieth century and the Myers-Briggs test (MBTI), which was widely used between the 1950s and 1990s. It is still used by many businesses today.

The Lumina Spark model is based on simplicity, and grounded in the solid empirical evidence base of the 'Big Five' approach to measuring personality traits.[14] I favour this approach because while it avoids the typing methodology that suggests you must be either an extrovert or an introvert (a challenge with popular systems like MBTI), it also shows how a combination of the aspects of your personality will lead to you having a tendency towards one of the four archetypes. This new approach to psychometrics was devised by Stewart Desson, a business psychologist. In its application of psychometrics in the business world, Lumina Spark has proved far more useful and effective. I have been using it for the past five years in my workshops, and clients find that having an understanding of the specific aspects of personality that their partners display, and the overall personality archetypes that they tend towards, makes a difference in their business and personal relationships. If you can get a grasp of the aspects of personality you have a preference for, and therefore the aspects that you use, you too will find you are able to 'speed read' your partner and therefore adapt and connect with more ease, and better outcomes.

The four archetypes and how they work

Although it deals with the complexity of the human personality, the Lumina Spark model is based on making a complex subject clear and accessible. You can use it yourself by simply looking at how the people you are negotiating with seem to fit in relation to those key areas that psychologists have shown are easy to measure. By outlining these eight aspects of personality (given below), and showing how they combine to form four colour archetypes that match the four sales types, I hope to give you access to an idea that you can use to build greater rapport and more collaborative partnerships.

The eight aspects of personality

What appeals to me about the model created by Stewart and his team is that you can easily understand these eight aspects and recognize them in yourself and others.

As you will see, each aspect of personality has an opposite, which is easily identified using the Lumina Spark model, shown in the image on page 108. However, it's important to remember that this does not make them mutually exclusive. The Lumina Spark approach treats each aspect independently. In the portraits we use in business, we test each aspect separately, using a series of questions. In this chapter I will show how, by understanding the eight aspects and how they combine to form the colours, you can find ways to see how your personality and that of your customer can best adapt and connect with each other.

1. Big-picture thinking – This is about creativity. Looking at things in a unique way, people with a high big picture thinking score are often visionaries. They look beyond the reality of 'what is' towards 'what could be'. They want to make improvements and shake up the status quo. These individuals will champion their ideas, even if it means introducing changes of dramatic proportions. In addition, they are not afraid to speak up, even if others may consider their ideas strange.

2. Down to earth – This is about knowing how to make projects manageable. People who are strong in this aspect dissect projects into smaller pieces and focus on the details. This attention to detail makes them very skilful at producing consistent and accurate work. They assess things in the light of their experience, preferring to utilize approaches that have worked for them in the past. They can be very even-minded and careful when accepting change initiatives and are likely to have a reputation for being more traditional in their methods.

3. Extroverted – This is about enjoying working alongside other people. Individuals who are strong in this aspect have no trouble approaching new people and telling them about their thoughts and ideas. They like to voice their opinions and to know that their voice is heard. People who score high on this aspect enjoy having new conversations just to see where they might lead. They can be demonstrative with their emotions in the sense that when they're happy everyone will notice and they often display their feelings openly. They can be seen as the life and soul of the party, exuding enthusiasm and always confident enough to speak up in a group.

4. Introverted – This person is likely to be seen as private and level-headed, with a desire to keep their feelings under wraps. This can make them appear quiet and serious. They will think before they voice their opinions or act upon ideas, especially when they are in a group setting. They are measured and take a serious approach to work, controlling any display of excitement. They produce great results when they can work independently, as they often do not find the opportunity to speak up in a crowd. They are listeners who take into consideration other people's ideas and input before offering their own opinions.

5. People-focused – This is visible in someone who is willing to adapt their stance to accommodate others. They're not overly outspoken and they avoid opportunities to express negative feedback. They are trustworthy and like to trust others. They seek harmony and approval from others – they may be known as 'peacemakers'. They acknowledge others in a team, and appreciate their contributions. They value other people's ideas but may be modest and uncomfortable with receiving praise themselves. They readily see the world from other people's perspectives, making them appear considerate and courteous.

6. Outcome-focused – This can apply to someone who is objective, rational, views themselves as successful and enjoys competition. When faced with a challenge they take the logical route and a direct approach to communication, which is very 'to the point'. They are not afraid of conflict and can be tough negotiators because they prioritize the outcome over other people's feelings. They are good at arguing their point in order to share their opinions. When others communicate with them, they will value their well-considered ideas. They dislike waffle.

7. Discipline-driven – This is evident in someone who utilizes self-discipline and demonstrates precision and punctuality. They tend to start work early and avoid last-minute deadlines. They take time management seriously – both their own and that of others. They think carefully before taking action and they take their commitments very seriously. They are very consistent in the application of their work ethic. They like to establish clear written objectives and work purposefully towards goals they have set. They are very organized and methodical, enjoying planning and scheduling what needs to be completed. They prefer to work in an ordered and structured environment.

8. Inspiration-driven – This is present in someone who is flexible and lets things emerge. They allow the work pace to develop naturally until a final objective becomes clear. They like to let the direction emerge from an evolving situation. They are easy-going and are able to work loosely with processes. They use their gut instinct to make quick choices, using the pressure of approaching deadlines to push them into action. They take risks by bending rules and traditions, in order to achieve something that will be unique.

TRY THIS NOW: Use the descriptions above to notice what preferences you think you have.

Give yourself a score between 1 and 10 for each of the aspects, where 1 means you see very little of yourself in an aspect and 10 means you feel it describes you exactly. Feel free to choose aspects that are seemingly opposite. Many people are able to use opposite qualities in different aspects of their life or at different times, so why not you?

If you are feeling that you have strengths in all areas, take a sense check. Are you really so well rounded that you are strong in all these areas? (If so, well done! There may be a role for you in the next *X-Men* movie!)

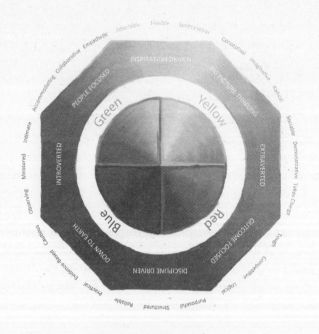

The four personality archetypes

Stepping back and looking at the complete image of our personalities painted by the eight aspects, you will also be able to see the four distinctive sales types.

The model doesn't suggest that you will fall neatly into one colour type. Rather, most people will contain elements of all four colours to varying degrees. By focusing on the details of the eight aspects of your own and your customer's personalities, and moving outwards to see the 'big picture' of the archetype, useful insights into your own and your customer's natures will emerge.

All four archetypes have their upsides and downsides, but none is necessarily better than the others or makes someone more effective or collaborative as a negotiator. It's only when a person overextends their strengths in one particular colour that it starts to become a weakness. By appreciating the differences between people, and by learning to read others, it's possible to adapt your negotiation style to best suit the kind of person you are collaborating with.

Conscientious Blue (the Analytical Influencer)

The blue archetype is defined by combining the following aspects of personality: introverted, down to earth and discipline-driven. This often leads to a person with highly tuned organization skills and high reliability and attention to detail. They are good listeners and observers and tend to make objective decisions based on the evidence at hand.

The downside: this tendency towards empiricism can sometimes take the form of fussy, bureaucratic leanings and this type can occasionally find themselves unable to make a decision due to 'information overload'.

The Analytical Influencer is highly motivated by detail, and factual elements of the deal. They reject personal approaches in the main and prefer to discuss tangible and practical details. They like to plan, so they are well-prepared buyers, although their tendency towards detail and their reflective qualities mean that they may need time to consider proposals, and they may get bogged down.

Selling to the Conscientious Blue
(the Analytical Influencer)

DO	DON'T
Be well prepared, and show it.	Try and wing it, or do things on the hoof.
Be prepared to share detail of your proposal if possible.	Be too 'big picture' in your approach – stick to the facts.
Stick to a process and communicate that you are doing so.	Change your plan too easily or get caught up with new ideas.
Establish clear timelines and be fastidious about sticking to them.	Try to introduce variables that are too creative, or unproven.
Provide practical data-driven examples of how the deal will work.	Speak too much or too quickly.

DO	DON'T
Listen carefully and allow plenty of time for reflection.	Try and make it too personal – keep your physical and emotional distance

Empowering Green (the Amiable Influencer)

The green archetype is defined by empathy and people skills. It combines the following personality aspects: introverted, people-focused and inspiration-driven. They work well with others and are able to appreciate multiple points of view. They are often perceived as a positive, calming influence within their organization.

The downside: this kind of sociability can make it difficult for them to function outside of a group dynamic and they may find themselves taking on more work than they can manage due to being unable to say 'no' to anyone.

The Amiable Influencer is motivated by people and co-operation, so will be interested in how the deal serves those around them. They will like to take a more co-operative approach so naturally will be more open and flexible. As they share the aspect of introversion with the Analytical Influencer they will also need time to reflect and won't like to be pushed into making fast decisions, especially as they will want to consult with others before deciding.

Selling to the Empowering Green
(the Amiable Influencer)

DO	DON'T
Focus on how the proposal will impact people.	Try to stick too rigidly to your plan.
Use real examples of the way people have benefited from your product or service.	Expect to move the process on too quickly.
Allow time to have more reflective and personal conversations during the process.	Use too much detail or factual information to persuade.
Plan for an element of flexibility and welcome collaboration.	Reveal too much of your competitive side (if you have one).
Listen and allow the person time to reflect.	Ignore the people involved in the process.
Include creative variables, particularly ones than benefit other people.	Be too direct or blunt.

Inspiring Yellow (the Expressive Influencer)

The yellow archetype is present in the 'fun' members of the office. It combines the following personality aspects: extroverted, big picture thinking and inspiration-driven. They're spontaneous, imaginative and often the ones who offer solutions no one else would have considered. They are socializers and adept at lightening the mood when necessary.

The downside: their fun-loving nature can work to their detriment, as they often show a tendency to be poorly organized and easily distracted.

New ideas and creative thinking motivate the Expressive Influencer. They enjoy the sales process when they are allowed to have input into making the deal different, and they enjoy engaging in the process and brainstorming together with you to solve obstacles along the way. They are inspired by new ideas, and are prepared to throw caution to the wind to try out those new ideas.

Selling to the Inspiring Yellow
(the Expressive Influencer)

DO	DON'T
Allow time for face-to-face discussion.	Focus too much on facts or details.
Be prepared to be flexible in your approach.	Expect them to read everything you've sent them.
Listen to and encourage their creativity.	Try and stick too rigidly to a structure.
Prepare yourself, but don't expect them to.	Ignore their ideas.
Start with the big idea, and allow them to buy into this first.	Present your idea as one that is already fixed.

DO	DON'T
Be descriptive and enthusiastic in your language and style.	Leave them with follow-up tasks that are not clearly defined.

Commanding Red (the Driving Influencer)

The red archetype is all about action. It combines the following personality aspects: extroverted, outcome-focused and discipline-driven. They are decision-makers and go-getters; usually the first to take charge in a group. They are highly competitive and motivated and will tend to go far in their chosen careers as a result.

The downside: this directness can come at the expense of social skills and they may be perceived by others as overly aggressive and insensitive.

The Driving Influencer likes to win and is more comfortable with conflict than many others. They like to get on with things at a fast pace and enjoy taking quick decisions in order to achieve their desired outcomes. While they are not naturally the most flexible or collaborative, if you can show them the value of cooperation, they will quickly get onboard.

Selling to the Commanding Red
(the Driving Influencer)

DO	DON'T
Move at a fast pace.	Get competitive and try to win an argument.

DO	DON'T
Stick to the facts.	Get annoyed if they keep you waiting or try to dominate you.
Focus on outcomes.	Get into too much detail.
Expect them to make fast decisions.	Be too conceptual, or focused on ideas.
Allow them to be in control of the pace of the sale.	Focus on feelings.
Show them the next steps and how to take them.	Expect them to involve too many others in the process of agreeing the deal.

TRY THIS NOW: Using your scores for each of the eight aspects from the exercise on page 108, combine them to see how much you regularly use each of the four colour archetypes. In completing both this and the previous exercise, when you were reflecting on what aspects of your personality were used most regularly, you may even want to focus on how you use these personalities when you are selling. If you've done the exercise in relation to your broader life, how do your general and commercial personalities differ?

Commanding Red Archetype – Driving Influencer

_____ Extrovert

_____ Outcome-focused

_____ Discipline-driven

_____ TOTAL

Conscientious Blue Archetype – Analytical Influencer

_____ Discipline-driven

_____ Down to earth

_____ Introvert

_____ TOTAL

Empowering Green Archetype – Amiable Influencer

_____ Introvert

_____ People-focused

_____ Inspiration-driven

_____ TOTAL

Inspiring Yellow Archetype – Expressive Influencer

_____ Inspiration-driven

_____ Big picture thinking

_____ Extrovert

_____ TOTAL

TRY THIS NOW: Think of a person you are negotiating with and go through each of the eight aspects of their personality. Mark them between 1 and 10 on how much you think they display each aspect. Using this information, list which two of the four colour archetypes are strongest in them.

> How does your use of the colour types compare to theirs? How may that cause tension when you are selling? What can you do to tune up or tone down an aspect of your personality to adapt more effectively with this partner?

The value of flexibility

The more you think about how to adapt and connect with others by focusing on the ways in which you are different, the easier you will find it to get on with people in many walks of life. Ultimately I have found that there are very few 'difficult' people, just 'different' people. Understanding these differences has helped me craft many relationships and agreements. I trust this kind of adaptive action will do the same for you.

It is worth noticing that the idea of a fixed personality that is with you forever and cannot be adjusted is not one that Desson's team at Lumina Learning has a lot of truck with. As part of a growing group of psychologists who take a 'humanistic' approach to psychology, they have produced evidence that suggests humans are able to adapt aspects of their personality. While there will always be other more traditional psychologists who look at your personality traits as something that are largely fixed from childhood, my experience is that every individual does have the ability to adjust aspects of their behaviour, regardless of the personality preferences they most commonly use. This flexible view is also supported by a recent study by Nathan Hudson and R. Chris Fraley of the University of Illinois at Urbana-Champaign. Their study produced evidence that, when motivated to do so, individuals could change specific aspects of their personality and boost their usage of other particular personality traits. Hence it seems that, with some effort, you can adjust your personality to the circumstances.[15]

CHECKLIST

— Are you clear how you use the eight aspects of your personality?

— Can you see which aspects of your personality you may use too much of in sales situations and therefore need to tone down?

— Can you see which of the four colours you use most in your sales interactions? Does this vary in different situations?

— Are you noticing how your buyer is using the eight aspects of their personality? Are they dominant in a particular colour type?

— How may you tone down (or tune up) certain aspects of your personality to connect more effectively with specific customers?

— How may you change the way you prepare and propose agreements to adapt your style to specific partners you have identified as different from you?

9:

THE SELLING STATE OF MIND

Why then 'tis none to you; for there's nothing
either good or bad, but thinking makes it so
– Hamlet (William Shakespeare)

When I was first in the selling business I took it very seriously. I had made it my 'profession', but some of the best operators had a slightly different attitude. My mentors at the time called it a 'game', but I didn't really understand. After over thirty years in the 'game' I now see what they mean. The more seriously you take it, the less you take from it. That's not to say you don't have to work hard, or do things to get results.

One of my first sales managers told me that a sale was 90 per cent perspiration, 10 per cent inspiration. He said that no matter how hard you worked, if you didn't have the right attitude you were bound to fail. He was right about the attitude, but it took me some time to realize he had got it the wrong way round. Truth is, I didn't notice him perspiring much: he seemed to love his job, and moved effortlessly in and out of sales engagements. He had the magic touch.

By the time I was managing my own sales teams, I realized that attitude made up far more than 10 per cent of the game. Without the right feeling on the sales floor, and the right attitude in the individual's selling, there was little point in connecting with customers. It was clear that a poor mood was a huge barrier to sales. We knew that to achieve results we needed to work on our mindset, as well as our skill set. Maybe it was 50 per cent mindset to 50 per cent skill set.

Once I became responsible for training salespeople I started to see the balance tipping the other way. Regardless of what people were taught, if they lacked confidence, or belief, they were still bound to fail. I started to explore ways to create the right mindset in salespeople. Having studied under masters in the field such as Paul McKenna, Richard Bandler, Antony Robbins and Michael Neill, I became very adept in the art and science of positive attitude. I learnt how to hypnotize people to 'forget' phobias and I mastered visualization techniques that helped me and others quickly enter peak performance states. I taught my participants what we called 'mindrobics' – exercises that would tone up the mind and point us towards more productive mental states. The success rate was variable, but as it was the best I could find to impact state of mind, I knew it was valuable and useful.

Then one day in 2010 I received a message from Jamie Smart, a fellow student of NLP, who had gone on to become one of the UK's leading NLP trainers. Through his mentor, Michael Neill, Jamie had stumbled across a new understanding of how the mind works, one that pointed away from all of the tools and techniques that attempted to change our thoughts. It is called the 'human operating system'.[16] I could see that what I was teaching was limited in its impact, and was keen to explore what Jamie had discovered. So I embarked on a learning journey that has uncovered new insights for me, and that I am excited to share with you in this chapter. The human operating system is the 'missing link' in sales success.

This isn't a book about insight principles, but I want to show how you can benefit from understanding the role played by your personal thinking in the sales process.[17] More importantly, I want to show how this understanding enables you to build deeper relationships. You'll realize how easy conversations can be once you have achieved a real connection with the other person. When you stop your personal thinking, you enter what sports people often refer to as 'the zone'. In this state of mind we connect to our customer at a much deeper level. We also connect to our own power base of knowledge, memory, and what my friend – a fellow i-Heart[18] associate – Ian Watson calls 'collective consciousness'.[19] Without the barrier created by personal thinking we have access to far more creativity, resourcefulness and potential impact. Garret Cramer, who works with top performers in the field of sport, calls this state 'still-power', and when we reach it our natural resources shine through, allowing us to get more from ourselves.[20]

There are two things you need to know in order to understand your own OS (operating system). First, that the mind only works one way, and second, that it is designed for success. Remember: the theory that your body is responding to your external circumstances is false. Your body can only ever respond to your thinking. It's how we work as humans.

Insight sales principle 1: Your mind only works one way

Can you really ever feel anything without a thought? We experience the whole world through the lens of our thinking, and are tricked into believing that what we are seeing is real. To quote Sydney Banks, 'Thought is not our reality; yet it is through thought that our realities are created.'[21]

We imagine that our brain is a camera, but in reality it is a projector, with some very cool effects at its disposal. We have in the gift of our thinking a special effects department that is on a Hollywood budget, and can produce unbelievable feelings. And when we think the circumstances are creating the feelings, we are simply being fooled. We are only ever feeling the effects of the projector; the circumstances themselves can't produce feelings, only thoughts. If we deepen our understanding of the inside-out nature of our reality, we will lose our attachments to negative feelings. This is a critical tool in sales. We sell when we are in the present; when we are in our heads we are not connected with others.

You don't need to become a Zen master, devoid of anxious thought, to be an effective persuader. You just need to know that anxious or fearsome feelings are natural, they are momentary, and they are a result of thinking rather than circumstances.

TRY THIS NOW: Take an object towards which you have no feelings (for example, a pen or a plastic cup) and place it in front of you. Take a look at it. Concentrate on it and notice how long you last until your thinking is distorted by another thought. If you think, *I wonder how long I've been going,* there is the new thought.

We have hundreds of thoughts, and when we attach too much meaning to them we begin to create problems for ourselves. As George Pransky, one of my teachers and author of *The Relationship Handbook*, says, 'Just because you have a thought, do you have to invite it in to have a cup of tea?'[22]

Insight sales principle 2: You have an innate design for success, which enables realization and insight

Many people in my training sessions have said 'so what?' when they first start to look in the direction of this understanding. Let's return to the FAB structure we used in Chapter 6 (see page 69) to explore further.

If thought is the **Feature**, awareness is the **Advantage**. Thought is a principle, a fact. The **Advantage** is that when you recognize that you are just experiencing your thought, you will see that a new thought is likely to come along soon. The **Benefit** of this is that you can easily put aside anxious thoughts and connect instead with more helpful, positive and empowering feelings.

You have already experienced this in your life. My mother would tell me to 'sleep on it' and that it would look different in the morning, and she was right. In teaching 'creativity' I discovered that when you germinate ideas, and let them fertilize in the realm of the unconscious, you will eventually reap new ideas that are way beyond your original thinking.

Why is this important in sales? It means that when you feel stuck, you are only ever one thought away from a new perspective and fresh ideas. It also means that your customer is as well. The implications of this will extend way past the remit of this book, but for now I'll just invite you to apply this learning to your sales conversations.

If you watch a great presenter, actor, sportsperson or raconteur at work, you will see they have one thing in common. They are truly present. They are in a state of mind where they are 100 per cent connected to their real power, and undistracted by their personal thinking. In this state of presence they are able to access all the resources they need for success. This is not a supernatural state – it is a natural state. It is literally the state in which you were born, and in which you lived until the boundaries of your personal thinking started to get in the way.

THINK ABOUT THIS: Have you ever accessed resources you didn't know you had? Where you performed against the odds? Chances are you acted from intuition, rather than planning or judgement. Knowing that this resource is waiting for you is a useful tool to remember in sales conversations.

Rapport is simply connecting with another human being without letting your personal thinking get in the way. You have to do very little in order to sell, except allow the natural connection to help you both access your deeper wisdom.

If you allow the natural process to flow, you will see what Damian Mark Smyth means by 'do nothing'.[23] He is pointing you towards the idea that in an anxious and distressed mood you won't get better ideas. Your best ideas and access to your most effective resources will come when your thinking is slowed right down, and you are connecting with your own understanding and experience.

Knowing that fresh new thinking is available at any time is not only refreshing, but practical and profitable too. Looking in this direction will give you new insights into your own experience and help you make sales. The 'selling state of mind' is not a set of mantras that will push you towards a positive mindset. It is not a set of practices that will encourage you to think differently. The 'selling state of mind' is an understanding of how your mind works. An understanding that any stress or anxiety you are feeling can only be momentary, created by thought, and can be replaced by understanding if you allow yourself to settle and connect with whoever you are with. As salespeople we meet with lots of different people every day. If we use this opportunity to genuinely connect, we will allow ourselves to benefit from the understanding and wisdom of those we serve, and help them to see their own wisdom too.

CHECKLIST

— Are you aware that knowledge and experience are worthless without the right state of mind?

— Can you see that bad feelings impact your ability to genuinely connect with others?

— Can you see that your feelings are not coming from your circumstances, but from your thinking?

— How much are you able to see that life really is 100 per cent an 'inside-out' job?

— Do you realize that whatever you are thinking now, you will have a new thought soon?

— Do you see that as your mood and awareness change, so does your thinking?

— Are you able to trust that if you allow yourself time to settle, you will have access to new and more productive thinking?

— Can you see that your thinking gets in the way of your rapport with others?

— Are you able to notice that when you have your most productive sales conversations, you are thinking less and connecting more?

CONCLUSION

Many people I meet with and speak to believe that selling is a dark art. This approach makes it difficult for them to engage with the process productively, even when their livelihoods depend on it.

I trust you have now got a sense that selling doesn't need to be heavy. Or dark. Once you see it as a positive way of understanding and fulfilling the needs of others, selling takes on a different quality. To both the seller and the buyer.

With this shift in perspective comes a quantum shift in behaviour. Selling becomes less about closing and more about opening, less about push and more about pull. It is an essential human activity, one that draws people together. When you adopt this approach, selling becomes more enjoyable and increasingly effortless. It becomes light.

I hope that by using the ideas in this book you gain confidence and see the importance that really caring about the needs of the other party has in both the process and practice of getting stuff sold. I trust you will find the structure that has helped so many thousands of my participants useful. If only because it reminds you that preparing, connecting and discovering needs are far more important than presenting your wares in so many sales scenarios. I know that if you use the tools in this book ethically you will be able to craft agreement through genuine conversation.

I also look forward to hearing how deepening your

understanding of the human operating system has helped you connect with others and with the source of your greatest strengths.

I wish you the best of luck in using these ideas in your personal and professional life. Remember: we are born light, and uniquely equipped to communicate with others. Selling can be a brilliant opportunity to tune into this fine human quality, to meet and connect with many incredible people and learn and grow in the process.

Acknowledgements

I can't list all the people who have helped me learn the art of selling, but a few stand out as particularly worthy as they gave me opportunities to hone my understanding. Dave and Hazel, of Worldwide Marketing, two of the best market/exhibition demonstrators in the world. Paul and Brian, street grafters from south London, who picked me up in Australia and honed my pitching skills and knowledge of business. David and the Margolis brothers, who showed me some light (and dark) arts in the business equipment world. My law lecturers for teaching me the art of logical argument. John, Fiona, Linda, Paul and all the team at MSM who showed me that passion produces results. My fellow mavericks Bruce and Kathleen, who plotted with me to be disruptive and yet still effective, and all the gang at MSM and Capital Radio. Tim, Tom and Karen and the whole team at Emap On Air. My mentors in the world of training, Paul and Mike, and the team at Apex who made it possible for me to learn. Ricardo and Elisa and all the DOOR International team for demonstrating what it means when we say 'people buy people first'. All those people who have helped me in my understanding of how the 'human operating system' really works, Jamie, Aaron, Mara, Michael, The Pranskys, Ken, Robin, Terri, Brian and all the Iheart and IHC Team. And the children of Rabbi Hagar's class at Hasmonean – you particularly inspire me by the way you live and learn. Steven and the Inspire team, who are the best people I know to bring this material alive. And every customer who has given me the privilege of training thousands of your people across the world. It is those participants that I want to thank the most. Every day I get to train, I learn more from your insight and your wisdom. Thank you all for your generosity of spirit and for being able to learn as you teach me.

Notes

1 *To Sell Is Human: The Surprising Truth About Moving Others*, Daniel Pink.

2 *SPIN Selling*, Neil Rackham.

3 *Don't Sweat the Small Stuff . . . and It's All Small Stuff*, Richard Carlson.

4 *The Missing Link: Reflections on Philosophy and Spirit*, Sydney Banks.

5 *Synchronicity: An Acausal Connecting Principle*, C. G. Jung.

6 *Louis Pasteur: the Vaccine Inventor: Life and work of the great scientist*, John Tyndall and René Vallery-Radot

7 *Blink: The Power Of Thinking Without Thinking*, Malcolm Gladwell.

8 *SPIN Selling*, Neil Rackham.

9 *Pre-Suasion: A Revolutionary Way To Influence and Persuade*, Robert Cialdini.

10 *Confessions of an Advertising Man*, David Ogilvy

11 *Influence: The Psychology of Persuasion*, Robert Cialdini.

12 *Results: Think Less, Achieve More*, Jamie Smart.

13 *Rejection Proof: How I Beat Fear and Became Invincible*, Jia Jiang

14 More information on the Lumina Spark model can be found at www.luminalearning.com/inspire, or you can download the Splash app on the Apple or Google app stores.

15 *Volitional Personality Trait Change: Can People Choose to Change Their Personality Traits?*, Nathan Hudson and R. Chris Fraley of the University of Illinois at Urbana-Champaign.

16 *Results: Think Less, Achieve More*, Jamie Smart.

17 *Invisible Power: Insight Principles at Work*, Dr Ken Manning, Robin Charbit and Sandra Krot.

18 iHeart Schools Programme, innate health and resilience training programme for schools, a project of The Innate Health Centre, www.innatehealth.com.

19 Ian Watson @ The Insight Space www.theinsightspace.com.

20 *Stillpower: Excellence With Ease in Sports and Life*, Garret Cramer.

21 *The Missing Link: Reflections on Philosophy and Spirit*, Sydney Banks.

22 *The Relationship Handbook*, George and Linda Pransky.

23 *Do Nothing! Stop Looking, Start Living*, Damian Mark Smyth.

Index